COMPLETE GUIDE TO THE HOTCHKISS MACHINE GUN

FIG. 1.

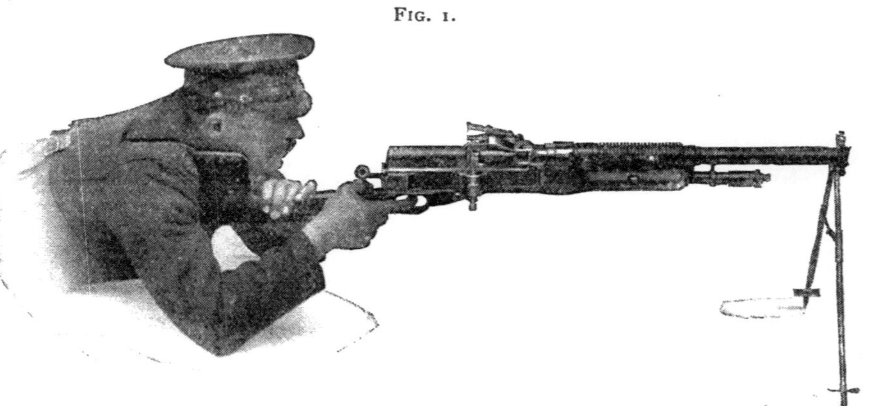

Firing position without elevating gear; shoulder strap opened and pressed down firmly against shoulder, left hand grasping stock.

Fig. 2.

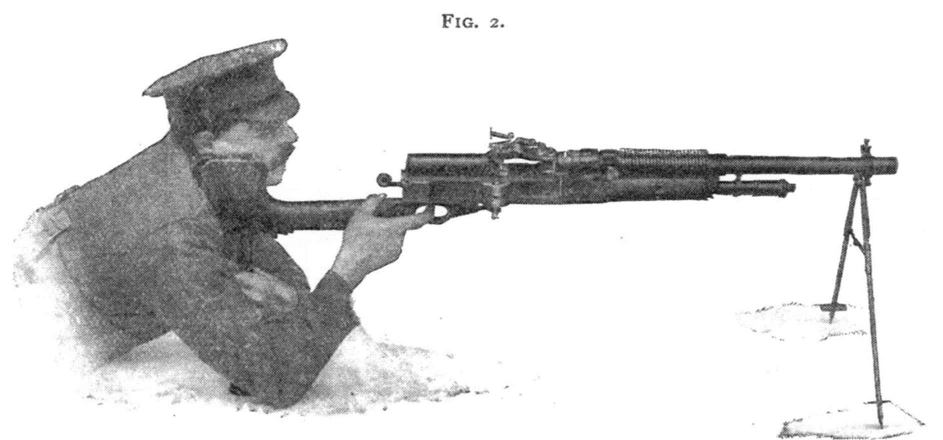

Firing position with elevating gear; shoulder strap folded down; left hand grasps outer elevating screw.

COMPLETE GUIDE

TO

THE HOTCHKISS MACHINE GUN

BY

AN INSTRUCTOR

LONDON:
GALE & POLDEN, LTD.
2 AMEN CORNER, PATERNOSTER ROW, E.C. 4
WELLINGTON WORKS, ALDERSHOT;
AND NELSON HOUSE, PORTSMOUTH.
Obtainable of all Booksellers.

PREFACE

In producing this book on the "Hotchkiss Portable Machine Gun," the Author wishes to express his appreciation and indebtedness for Instruction received at the Southern Command School of Musketry, Hayling Island, and for "Refreshers" by its Travelling School, and ventures to hope the knowledge thus gained, and now published, may prove of use to Machine Gun Sections.

From experience gained in instructing, one cannot emphasize strongly enough the need for the "proper handling" of a machine gun.

This can only be gained by strict attention to drill.

The great tendency is to become careless over movements, and to develop speed at the expense of accuracy.

This must be carefully watched and immediately checked in the training of a machine gun section.

Each gunner should be allowed to strip and assemble the gun himself, and so become familiar with the mechanism and every part of the gun.

The best method of testing his knowledge of the

working of the gun is to ask him to explain to the rest of the section, from time to time—(1) stripping and assembling in detail; (2) mechanism of gun; (3) adjustment of gas regulator; (4) I.A. and stoppages; (5) points before, during, and after firing; (6) care and cleaning.

All connected with machine guns should become so familiar with the gun that it should become almost an instinct to manipulate or fire the gun, to deal with all stoppages, and the application of immediate action.

It is desirable that machine gun instructors should qualify to take their sections in Physical Training, as it keeps the section "lively," enthusiastic, and interested (so necessary to secure the regular attendance, especially of Volunteers, with so many professional and business duties to occupy their minds).

The "quickening exercises" taught in P.T. are invaluable in making a gun section smart in their drill. These executive actions, in which the co-ordination of brain and muscle are brought into sympathy with one another, make for quickness in action, and presence of mind is developed.

Games for use with P.T. appeal to the soldier, and not only make him supple in body, but it is a form of brain drill, working in order to liven the mind. The ideal is to get the men to look forward to their drills with keenness, and the aim of those in command of machine gun sections should be to make this section the smartest in the battalion.

Signals for the control and observation of fire should not only be taught, but the section constantly practised in semaphore and the code used in signalling the results of observation of fire.

I have to acknowledge my indebtedness to the Hotchkiss et Cie. for kindly allowing me to have their illustrations of the gun, and their kindness when visiting their works.

F. W. B.

LEAMINGTON.

CONTENTS

LIST OF ILLUSTRATIONS

FIG. 3.

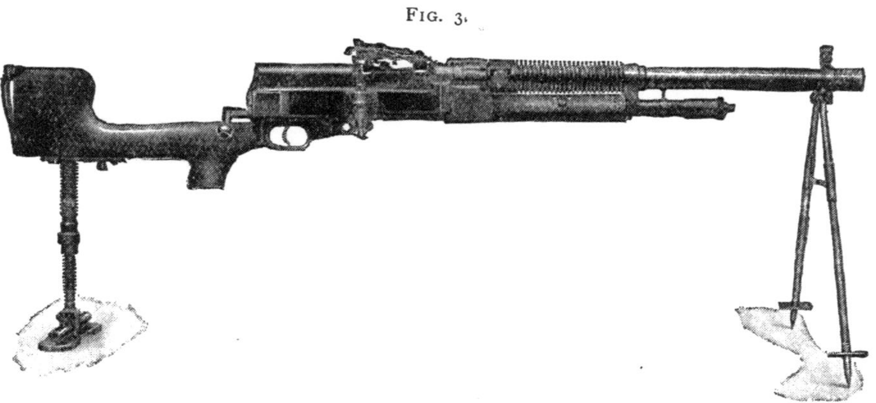

Infantry Model with Elevating Gear.

COMPLETE GUIDE TO THE HOTCHKISS MACHINE GUN

CHAPTER I

GENERAL DESCRIPTION

1. THE Hotchkiss Portable Machine Gun, or Automatic Rifle, possesses a great reserve of fire, is of wonderful possibilities, quick in action, light in weight, and simplicity of construction.

2. **Few Parts.**

There are only twenty-six component parts, divided into two groups—*external* (black), *working* (bright).

3. **Origin.**

The principle of *all* gas operated machine guns is of Austrian invention, the inventor's name being Colonel Odkelick; and as the outcome of this invention the Hotchkiss et Cie., of Paris and Coventry, produced their guns, which are now used by the British Cavalry, in the Tanks, and by both the French and Belgian Armies.

4. **Weight.**

The weight of the gun is about 28 pounds, including the folding barrel rest, which weighs about $1\frac{1}{2}$ pounds, and is used for steadying the gun when firing in the prone position, which will be ordinarily taken (see frontispiece).

For aircraft the gun is mounted on a crutch, and the stock replaced by a pistol grip.

5. **Cooling.**

The gun is cooled by air, and not by water, this being an advantage, as water is not always easily obtainable.

The radiator is on the barrel, and comprises flanges, giving the barrel a larger cooling surface.

6. **Rate of Fire.**

The gun fires at the rate of **600** rounds per minute.

Automatic.—With two men, the speed of fire is **400** rounds per minute, but with one man, who loads and fires, the rate of fire is **250** rounds per minute.

Repetition.—At repetition single shots only are fired, at the rate of 100 per minute.

7. **Principle of Gun.**

The gun is operated automatically by two forces :

(1) The pressure of gas resulting from the explosion of the charge.

(2) The recoil spring.

Guided in the receiver parallel to and below the barrel is the piston, which by its reciprocating motion assures the automatic action of the gun. It is brought about as follows:

When the bullet in its passage through the bore has passed a part connecting the barrel with the gas cylinder, a small portion of the powder gas, trapped, issues from the nozzle, and, impinging in the cup-shaped forward extremity of the piston, drives it to the rear. The recoil spring, compressed by the piston in its rearward movement, now drives the piston again to its initial position.

8. **Feed Strips.**

The cartridges are fed into the gun on flat tempered steel strips, of 30 rounds each.

The strips, empty, weigh about $4\frac{1}{2}$ ounces; when full, about 1 pound 15 ounces. There are also strips of 9 usually carried in bandoliers, and special arrangements are made for the 14 round strips.

New strips have now been introduced in the form of a belt. These are made up of "three round" links, except the first link, which is a "six round" link to facilitate introduction in receiver; it is made to take 50 rounds used in the Tanks).

9. **Ammunition Boxes.**

These contain 10 feed strips of 30 rounds each, filled by hand or by a filling machine.

10. **Butt Stocks.**

The ordinary rifle butt stock may be used, which enables the firer to keep a good hold on the gun and to fire it with ease from the shoulder; but the butt stock can be replaced by a pistol grip for general use in confined positions, such as a Tank, where it is required to reduce the length of the gun, the space in the Tanks being very restricted.

11. **Grouping.**

The absence of recoil enables a novice to obtain an excellent group on any target. This is a decided advantage, as in the case of some machine guns much experience and practice in holding is absolutely necessary.

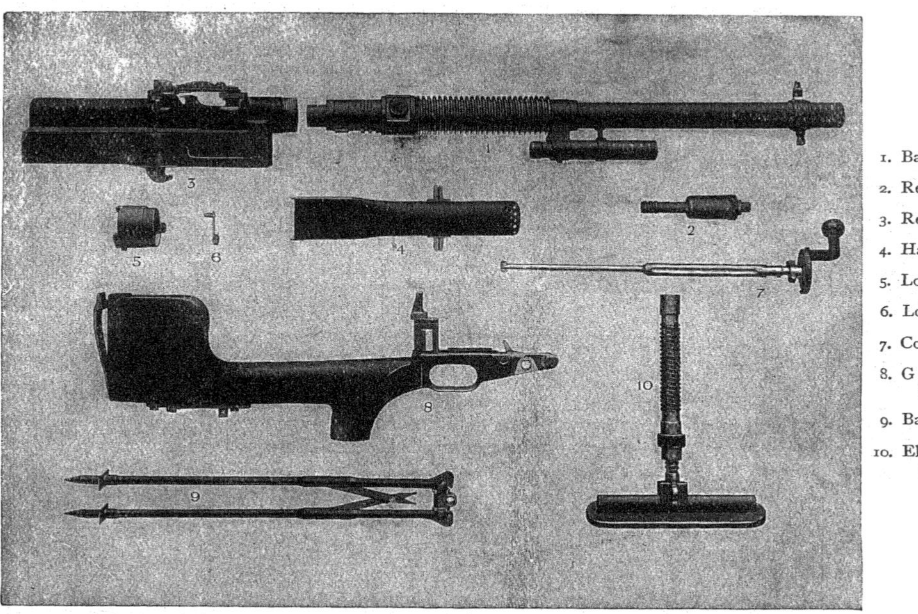

1. Barrel.
2. Regulator.
3. Receiver.
4. Hand Guard.
5. Locking Nut.
6. Locking Screw.
7. Cocking Handle.
8. Guard with Stock.
9. Barrel Rest.
10. Elevating Mechanism.

External Parts.

CHAPTER II

NOMENCLATURE OF PARTS OF THE GUN

Stationary Portion.

EXTERNAL.

THE stationary portion consists of: (1) Barrel, with gas cylinder; (2) receiver; (3) hand guard; (4) locking nut; (5) cocking handle; (6) guard and stock, with locking screw, and containing trigger mechanism; (7) barrel rest.

Barrel.

Brown in colour, to prevent rust. Is very thick and heavy, so that it gets hot less quickly. Made of mild steel. Muzzle counter-sunk, to prevent damage.

Fore Sight Carrier Ring (driven on and riveted).—Barley-corn sight, dovetailed into the foresight carrier and protected by hood. Underneath there is a projection for the bipod rest, which weighs 1½ pounds, and has shoes at ends and separators. The projection or bipod boss is flattened on one side to enable one to take the bipod off.

We next come to the—

Gas Nozzle Ring (driven on and riveted).—It holds the gas cylinder, the gas vent being carried through the ring and the extension. It also forms the gas cylinder support.

In advance of this you have a second support for the gas cylinder.

Cooling.—Behind the gas nozzle ring you have twenty-five flanges, which give a large cooling surface for the air, and form a radiator. Flat underneath for hand guard.

Trunnions.—These are not used now. Originally these were for elevating mechanism, or for use by cavalry or for aircraft, used on a crutch. They can be used in Tanks, and in this case the butt stock is substituted by a pistol grip.

In the rear of the trunnions are the arrangements for attaching the barrel to the receiver. These consist of a *key* formed on the underside of the barrel which enters a slot in the forward end of the receiver, thus positioning the barrel. You have a double set of interrupted flanges, which correspond with similar flanges in the locking nut; and a *stud*, under the left trunnion, which prevents the barrel entering too far into the receiver. The rear end of the barrel has recesses for the extractor claw and for the projectiles on the face of the breech block, cut for cartridge guide and bullet to enter.

Bore of gun same as rifle, five grooves, $\frac{1}{10}$ right over to left. Uniform; takes ·303 inch ammunition.

Gas Cylinder.—Is held to the barrel by nozzle ring and cylinder support. It consists of a tube into which the gas vent leads. Inside gas cylinder it is threaded; on right side graduated markings—o to $4\frac{1}{2}$ (5's) 45 in—for purposes of regulating size of gas cylinder. It is well to note: greater space, least gas force; confined space, greater the gas power.

Screwed into the gas cylinder, and adjustable to same, is a regulator piston.

On centre part of piston end there are three annular grooves, which when adjusted determine the amount of gas or pressure to be exerted on the piston.

The outer part of sleeve has a milled head portion for gripping when adjusting, also squared part for spanner use when barrel is hot. This fits over the gas cylinder and has two longitudinal saw cuts, the piece between the cuts being sprung inwards and provided with a nib, which engages in the channel in the gas cylinder and holds the regulator in position.

Orifice Screw.—Fits into orifice hole. The gas vent in barrel corresponds with hole of orifice screw. The screw must not be moved. It is there for manufacturing purposes. Carbon deposits can be removed from the vent by removing gas regulator and firing one or two rounds for this purpose.

In the rear end of the gas cylinder is a passage (nozzle) through which the gases pass on to the cup-shaped head of the piston.

Barrel Locking Nut.—This is attached to the front end of the receiver, and screws on to the barrel to keep the barrel fixed on to the receiver. *Outside* spring steel projection, provided with undercut serrations or teeth, which engage in the serrations or teeth on the receiver and save accidental rotation when firing. In front are two recesses to take the dismounting wrench for dismounting and assembling. Left of recesses you find hand guard stop, which engages the right shoulder of hand guard and holds hand guard into position. Barrel stop limits movement of barrel in locking nut. Inside barrel locking nut are three sets of interrupted flanges; these fit into corresponding flanges on the breech end of barrel, and the deep cut threads inside engage on corresponding threads on receiver.

Line on top indicates position of B.L.N. to strip.

Receiver.

Is of steel. It may be termed the most important portion of the gun, being practically the home or housing of the most essential working parts.

It forms the body of the gun, and consists of two portions, the upper and lower. The upper portion is *cylindrical* and the lower portion *rectangular* in shape. At the front end the cylindrical portion is threaded externally to take the *locking nut*, and a slot is cut underneath for the key on the barrel. Further to the rear this slot is enlarged to allow of the movement of the boss on the fermeture nut. *Externally*, in rear of the thread, is a small lug with serrations which engage with serrations on the *spring* of the locking nut.

On the rectangular part are the two slots in which the rear end of the hand guard engages.

Top of Receiver.—There are serrations; these engage the teeth under the steel spring projection of the barrel locking nut, and so prevent the vibration of the gun in firing. You also have on the top the guide line to indicate the position of the barrel locking nut for stripping and assembling the barrel.

Radial **Back Sight** graduated in 50 yards, 100 to 2,000 yards—even numbers on the right, odd numbers on left (Battle Sight). Normal range 900 yards. It is hinged at the rear of backside bed (a **V** sighting). It is adjustable by means of a slide with spring catches. A spring in bed of back sight supplies the rigidity necessary to hold the leaf on the ramps of back sight. The two ramps are for protection. The big screw fastens bed of back sight to the receiver, and is commonly called the lazy screw, being always in bed.

Feed Guides consist of guides front and rear, in which the cartridges travel, while grooves are cut in the upper portion to guide the strip. Between the feed guides is a wedge-shaped blade or tongue, its function being to force each cartridge slightly out of the strips as they come opposite the chamber.

Slot for Feed Piece.—In line to the right, and behind back sight hinge is a recess; into this recess the feed piece rests when the strip is absent.

Feed Spring Slot.—At the front, in line to the right of end of back sight, is a recess for feed spring, which holds the front of feed spring in its position.

Right Side of Receiver you have the housing for feed mechanism. It is closed by a spring-hinged cover; the flat spring keeps it closed, and a stud or button facilitates its opening. In this housing, which encloses the two arms of feed piece, there is a hole in the lower part which forms a bearing for the stem of feed piece, and allows its lower portion to pass through the bottom of the housing.

The Ejector and Spring.—Just above the feed piece housing is the ejector cap, with a cut recess for screw. This is the seating for the ejector, which is a small plunger, which, with its spring, is retained in the receiver by the screw cap, and projects into its interior.

Feed Strip Guides.—Shaped for front and rear feed guides; the rear one is slightly under for the base of the cartridge. Through the lower portion the cartridges travel, while grooves are cut in the upper portion to guide the strip.

Left Side.—Is the ejector opening, through which the cartridge cases are ejected. The ejector opening gives one a full view of the working parts.

Cartridge Stop.—On the top of the ejector opening, in the rear of same, and through the base of the wedge-shaped tongue, is drilled the recess for the cartridge stop and spring. It consists of a small plunger, surrounded by a spiral spring, in a cylindrical casing which screws into the tongue. It prevents cartridge going through, and indicates when gun is loaded.

Wedged-shaped Blade or Tongue.—This is between the guides, and projects from the left side of the breech casing, its function being to force each cartridge slightly out of the clips on the strips as they come opposite the chamber. The blade is waved; its centre is a raised rounded section engaging in the steel groove on the flat side of strip.

Guard Locking Screw.—For locking trigger guard and stock to the receiver; handle with milled head, for screwing and unscrewing. Small recess fits projection under the milled head.

Cocking Lever Stop Stud.—This stops the disc of the cocking lever in its rotation to the left.

Also printed on the left side is the title, number of gun, and calibre.

Bottom of receiver is riveted on, and has on it two hooks, which take the trunnions at the front end of guard. It is also hollowed out between hooks for easy play. Also recess for clearance of trigger guard, and to clear sear stop. In rear half no floor. This is formed by the guard itself.

Interior of Receiver.—On the upper surface of the roof of the cylindrical portion is a straight cam groove about 4½ inches on the straight, inclining at 25 degrees to the right for about 2 inches as it nears the top of the ejector opening. This takes the lug on the top of firing pin, and in this groove it rotates to the right.

The right side of this groove is continued to the rear end of the breech casing in the shape of a ridge, which keeps the upper boss on the firing pin in the recess in the breech block during that part of its travels.

Breech block ways, right and left, guides for flanges of the breech block, allowing them to move freely without binding on the piston.

At its rear end are the recesses into which the projections on the side of the guard engage, and the left side is drilled to take the screw which locks the rear end of the guard. The rear face has a portion of a circular groove which forms a path for the projection on the disc of the cocking handle.

Recoil Spring.—A coiled steel spiral spring which plays an important part in working the gun. There are 47 coils and a pressure of about 50 pounds. It lies in the interior of the piston rod. Its front end bears against the collar in the piston rod, and its rear end against the recess in the guard.

Hand Guard.

Is a casing of sheet steel, and fits forward end of receiver, and is the housing of the piston. At front end there are perforations for gas escape, allowing gases after actuating the piston to exhaust into the air. Gases escape through holes at the side. To it are riveted the spring clips which retain the legs of the bipod muzzle rest when it is not in use. Flattened on top to fit flat portion of the flanges (radiator) of barrel. Slot at bottom prevents guard from splitting by expansion. The two flanges on rear engage with the hand guard, and prevent falling off. The slit clears prolongation of piston.

Guard and Stock.

Joined together by two big screws and held into position by bolt. Guard itself recessed to allow for the trigger mechanism. Forward end, trunnions for hooks on bottom plate of receiver, and kept into position by a locking screw.

Hole for Spanish mounting. First projection is the sear stop, which limits the forward rotation of sear. The sear consists of a rotatable axis pin, carrying a block, which engages with a recess in the bottom of the piston rod, holding the latter back and thus performing the function of the nose of the sear in the rifle; an upright arm near the left end of the axis, which is engaged by the hook of the T-shaped arm; a downwardly projecting arm to which the other end of the spiral spring is attached; and, at the left extremity of the axis, a milled head, which can be used if the mechanism fails, or for the purpose of stripping and assembling.

There is a flat portion on the axis to allow the sear to be removed from the guard. The block is also cut away for this purpose.

Right side of guard you have piston bearings. At the end is the standard or rear wall of the guard.

Two flanges support wall of receiver. Hole cut for movable notched ring or floating collar. Opening takes shank of cocking handle.

Recess on side takes tail of trigger, shaped to fit rear end of receiver. Two lugs fit inside recesses.

Inside rear end of receiver has number of gun barrel.

Inside the rear wall is a floating collar; the collar has two *nibs*, which project inwards and engage the grooves on the cocking handle; while its rear face has several recesses which the nibs of the cocking handle engage, and they retain the cocking handle in its several positions. The forward portion of the recess serves to contain the rear end of the recoil spring, which bears against the collar and keeps it forced backwards. The cocking handle does not rotate unless force is applied to the lever.

Under the recess is a rectangular hole, which allows the tail of the trigger bar to pass through the guard arc lines, to indicate position of cocking lever.

Butt, one solid block of wood.

Hinged shoulder strap, hinged with a spring to go over shoulder.

In the absence of the elevating mechanism the hole in the butt is now utilized to hold an oil bottle; this is closed by a milled head, to which a brush is attached.

Cocking Handle.

Two pieces of metal riveted together, and consists of the lever and knob, circular plate or disc, and stem or shank. The lever springs backwards from the disc, and is then bent at right angles. On the shank there is an anchor used to remove inside mechanism. The disc has on its periphery, close to the lever, a projection which prevents the handle being turned over too far to the left. There are three lines at the back, marked respectively—

"A.," deep, automatic, bursts of fire.
"R.," shallow, repetition, or single shots.
"S.," safety.
Scribe marks.
("Auto.," "Rep.," "Safety," "Dismounting"),

and recesses diametrically opposite to the first two of these lines.

On the stem near the disc are two tenons, which work in the space between the rear face of the guard and the collar which it contains. On the front of these tenons are nibs, which engage with the recesses in the rear face of the collar and prevent the cocking handle rotating from set position.

On the stem are six longitudinal grooves. Of these, two are for lightness; the others are in two pairs: one open at the rear end and closed at the front, the other closed at the rear and open at the front.

At rear end these grooves fit into projecting nibs of the collar in the guard.

Circular groove fits on rear guard or wall of receiver.

Knob of Cocking Handle for Working.—On the base edges of the disc, slightly right, are two cut recesses, a deep and shallow one, through which the tail of trigger passes.

Working Parts.

Trigger Mechanism.

We will deal with this separately, as the trigger mechanism is never stripped except by N.C.O. for cleaning or repairs.

It consists of trigger with upper arm and lower arm and wedge-shaped tail, in one piece of cold steel forging.

The hook on the upper arm to catch step on the vertical arm of sear.

The tail, or fire regulator, of the trigger is a flattened blade of steel with a raised centre rib; this comes in recess of rear wall of guard, the disc of the cocking handle.

This fire regulator has a small pin attached to sear spring.

Both trigger and sear fit into the housing.

Sear.

Consists of a rotatable axis pin, carrying a block, with nose, which engages with a recess, or bent, in the bottom of the piston, holding the latter back and thus acting as the nose of the sear does in a rifle.

An upright or vertical arm has on it a step, which is engaged by the hook of the T-shaped arm (upper

Fig. 5.

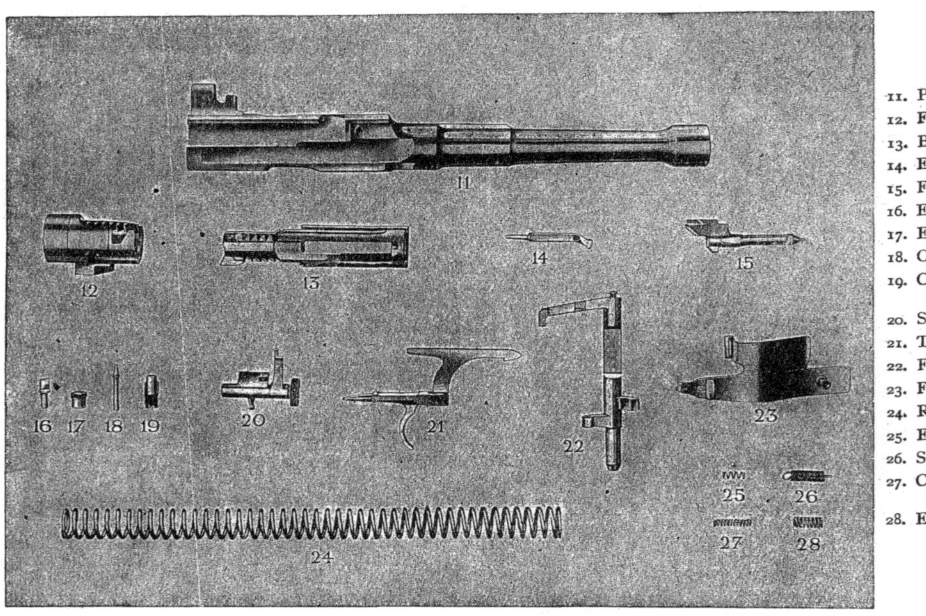

11. Piston.
12. Fermeture Nut.
13. Breech Block.
14. Extractor.
15. Firing Pin.
16. Ejector.
17. Ejector Cap.
18. Cartridge Stop.
19. Cartridge Stop Holder.
20. Sear.
21. Trigger.
22. Feed Piece.
23. Feed Spring.
24. Recoil Spring.
25. Ejector Spring.
26. Sear Spring.
27. Cartridge Stop Spring.
28. Extractor Spring.

Working Parts.

arm of trigger); a downwardly projecting arm to which the other end of the spiral spring is attached; and at the left extremity of the axis is a milled head for stripping and assembling, or in case of failure of the mechanism it can actuate the sear, and allows it to be rotated and the piston released. Between the block and the arm it is flat on the axis, which allows the sear to be removed from the guard, the block being cut away for this purpose.

Sear spring, attached to eyelet, into which spring fits.

Piston.

Is a heavy steel rod.

Front.—At the front end is the cup of piston, a hollowed end which fits on to or over the gas cylinder nozzle. Into this cupped head the spent gases strike, driving the piston to the rear.

Centre of piston is bored cylindrically, the hole being of sufficient diameter to take the front part of recoil spring. It forms, therefore, the seating of recoil spring.

About the centre is the bushing; a collar is there, and on this collar are two recesses cut in it to allow the lugs or anchor at the end of stem of cocking handle to fit, for pulling back the working parts.

Piston is numbered.

On Top of piston is a cam groove which actuates the fermeture nut when gun is working, the front face of the cam, as it moves back, unlocking the breech, and the rear face of the cam, as it moves forward, locking it.

Behind this is a block or lug, in which is a recess in which fits fang or lug on the bottom of firing pin. The large portion is rounded, enabling firing pin to rotate easily.

Body of Piston.—On this you have four flanges, which work in the rectangular portion of receiver and hand guard.

Underneath clean cut away, for clearance of firing and trigger mechanism.

The *bent* is cut to engage on trigger sear, and the front is inclined to engage sear.

Right Side are two ramps, upper and lower, inclined planes; these actuate feed mechanism. Situated at the base, on the front of piston flange, is the *shoulder;* this is utilized to keep the piston in its rearmost position and the breech open when the last of the strip has been fired. The holding back of the piston is accomplished by the shoulder; as it is held by the lower arm of feed piece, when the feed piece is forced down by spring to its lowest position, the gun is thus automatically placed at safety, the breech open, but not loaded.

Left Side of piston, its surface is cut away for clearance only, to allow projecting hooked arm of the trigger and the vertical arm of sear free play.

Breech Block.

It is cylindrical, with a flat surface, with flanges underneath its rear half to work in the guide grooves and to support it.

Top.—On the top you have a long and short recess. The firing pin, when assembled, fits into this short recess over to the left, the upper boss on the firing pin resting behind the shoulder.

Right Side you have a tapered groove which allows the breech block to pass the ejector in its forward movement. You have the reverse action in the backward movement, as the empty case strikes the ejector—hence ejector groove inclined.

Left Side.—Recess for extractor and spring, and hood for extractor, which holds the extractor in place. This prevents the claw of extractor rising too high, and allows claw to retain its grip over cartridge rim.

Front.—Interrupted threads. These engage in similar threads in the fermeture nut, locking and unlocking the breech.

Face.—On the face is the firing pin hole, to take the point of the firing pin, while the bolt head carries the hood which holds the extractor in place, and two projections which enter recesses in the rear face of the barrel.

Base.—On the base you have the recess to fit over the tang at rear of piston.

Fermeture Nut.

Is a steel sleeve. Internally you have an interrupted screw thread, corresponding with that on the breech block. Its forward portion is cylindrical and fits over the rear part of the barrel, and prevents forward movement of the fermeture nut, and its backward movement is made impossible by the shoulder in the receiver. It has two longitudinal slots cut in it: the upper, when in the unlocked position, allows the cartridge to pass from the strip to the chamber; the lower corresponds with the ejection opening in receiver. This slot is also recessed to allow hood of extractor to pass. You also have a depression which allows the front clips of the strip to pass.

Base.—Underneath you have a boss with two sloping sides; this is operated by the cam grooves in the centre on upper surface of piston, causing the nut to rotate. The little recess inside is a bed to catch brass filings.

Firing Pin.

Is cylindrical, and has underneath it a boss which engages in the tang recess on the top of piston when gun is assembled.

Top.—On top is the cam, which works along the upper inside cylindrical surface of the receiver; when to the left, it fits behind the shoulder of breech block. It is pointed at its extreme front end to strike the cap of cartridge.

The lower boss is also sloped at the rear end, to allow the removal of firing pin from breech block.

Feed Piece.

Consists of a *stem*, with partly flattened axis, to allow of its removal from its upper bearing through the narrowed division in line and above the feed piece housing. The stem has on its upper end a small undercut *stud*, which engages with the aperture in the feed spring. Below this is the *lever*, a flat square, tapering, with a square edge *pawl*, underneath, inclining to the left, and therefore so shaped as to engage the central openings in the strip, and so that it can ride over the ridges between the openings when the lever moves to the right. Below this the stem has the two flats, for removal (as explained), and towards the bottom are the *two arms*, which work by the cams on the right side of piston in the backward and forward movement, and allow the lever to perform its feeding motion from right to left.

The bottom of the stem passes through a hole in the feed piece housing, so that it can be pressed upwards for loading.

Feed Spring.

This is a shaped or curved spring from a flat steel plate. At its front end a *tongue* is formed to fit into the undercut recess on the front feed guide. The stud is to aid removal when stripping and replacing in assembling.

At the rear end of feed spring, on its right, is an aperture which fits over undercut stud on the stem of feed piece. In front of this is a *stud*, against which the front of undercut stud bears.

In the rear of the aperture the spring is curved downwards, to allow a means for removal, by the trigger pressing finger, to aid the easing of the spring from the stud.

On the left the spring is curved downwards, and provided with a *tooth* which engages with the rear openings in the strip and stops any movement of the strip to the right when the lever is moved in the same direction. The sloping face on the tooth allows it to slide over the ridges between openings when strip is moved to the left.

Bipod.

Is the means of steadying the gun when firing. It consists of a socket which is attached to a stud underneath the muzzle end of barrel.

On the inside, or the nearest to the barrel, are War Office markings and numberings. There are two hinged legs, between which are separators which hold rigid the extended legs, keeping them extended when in use. When folded, the legs are held by catches on the hand guard. Plates are on the lower ends of legs to prevent them being forced into the ground unequally. The plates are about 2 inches up the leg, and prevent the bipod from sinking into soft ground.

Springs of gun, other than those dealt with, are—

Sear Spring.—This connects sear and trigger in the trigger mechanism. Its action is extension and reverse pull, with hooks to connect sear and trigger.

Fig. 6.

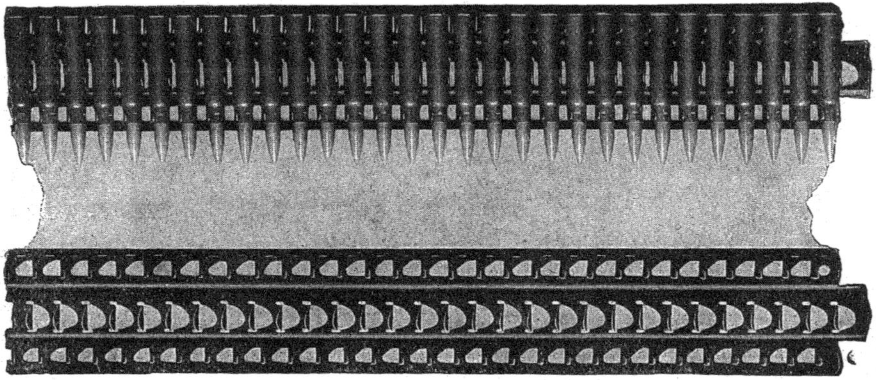

Feed Strip.

Extractor Spring.—In shape the *thickest* of small springs.

Ejector Spring.—*Smallest* of the small springs.

Cartridge Spring.—*Longest* of the small springs.

Feed Strips.

The cartridges are fed into the gun on these flat tempered steel strips. They are stamped from a single piece of flat sheet steel, and afterwards spring tempered so that the clips may have the desired elasticity. The strips hold 30 rounds each. There are three rows of clips, which hold the cartridge near the base, the middle, and at the neck. A stop lug which catches behind the head of the cartridge case prevents longitudinal motion.

Empty, strips weigh about 4½ ounces; full, about 1 pound 15 ounces.

There are also strips of 9, usually carried in bandoliers, and for the 14 round strips.

A *New Strip* has now been introduced in the form of a belt. These are made up of ***three round links***, except the *first link*, which is a *six round* link, to facilitate introduction in receiver. It is made to take 50 rounds, and is used in the Tanks.

To Clean.—Brush thoroughly and remove dirt and dust; better not use oil, but blacklead. This makes a good slipping surface.

Ammunition Boxes.

Ammunition boxes contain 10 feed strips of 30 rounds each, filled by hand or by a filling machine. Boxes are carried in the limber.

Feed Strip Filling Machine or Hopper.

Is constructed for clamping to a bench or plank, as, for instance, the lid of a cartridge box.

The hopper and clamp are removable for compactness in packing.

The machine must be so placed that the crank can be conveniently turned with the right hand.

Proceed as follows:

(*a*) Fill the hopper with cartridges.

(*b*) Push a feed strip, stop lugs to the rear, in the guides on the machine until the feed tooth catches back of the first middle clip.

(*c*) Turn the crank. At each complete turn of the clamp, first a cartridge is pushed forward into the clips, and then the feed strip fed ahead one notch into position for the succeeding cartridge.

(*d*) When filled, remove the strip.

This machine is operated most efficiently by two men. One supplies the machine with feed strips, turns the crank, and removes filled strips; the other supplies the hopper with cartridges.

Fig. 7.

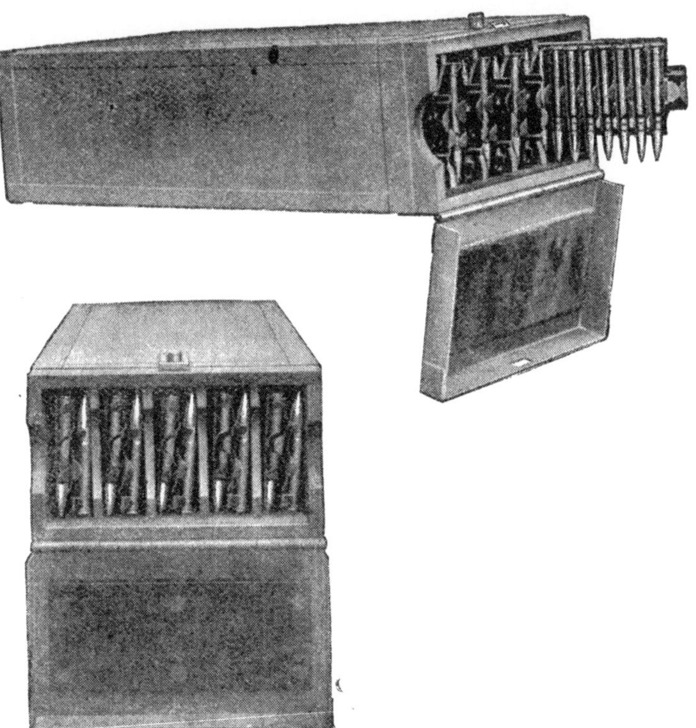

Ammunition Boxes.

Fig. 8.

Feed Strip Filling Machine or Hopper.

FIG. 9.

Resizing Tool.

FIG. 10.

Tripod Mounting.

Resizing Tool.

When the feed strips have been used repeatedly, the middle clips sometimes lose their curvature to such an extent that the cartridges are not firmly held. This is quickly remedied by passing the strip through the resizing tool, so as to restore the middle clips to their original form.

As a rule, very little resizing is necessary, slight contact between the resizing roller and the top of the middle clip sufficing.

So as to meet all cases, the resizing roller is made adjustable for height. It should be set progressively by trial by means of the six set screws provided for this purpose.

Tripod Mounting.

Consists of an aluminium yoke, grooved on either side to take the trunnions on barrel, and fitted with spring catches to retain them, pivoted in a saddle, and fixed by a screw with a vice pin. Underneath it is jointed to the upper end of a pivot which gives *horizontal traverse*, and is fixed by a clamping screw.

A *vertical pillar* passes through the leg bracket, and can be fixed at any height by means of a clamping screw.

Legs are hinged, their lower ends pointed, and with feet to rest in the ground.

A movable collar, actuated by a spring, presses the legs out automatically.

FIG. 11.

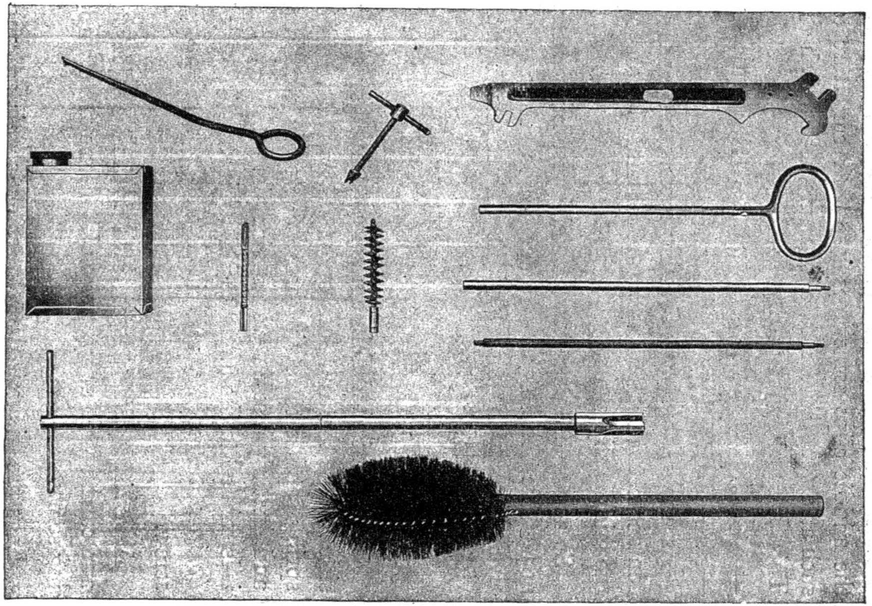

Accessories.

When not in use the lower part of tripod hinges forward under the gun, the legs being secured by a shackle, which passes round the gas cylinder. Between the ring and the gas cylinder support a brass chain passes round the legs and holds them.

Accessories.

One dismounting wrench.
One ejector key.
One hand extractor.
One cleaning rod complete.
Two wire brushes.
One cleaning brush.
One gas cylinder cleaner.
One oil can.
One front sight cover.

CHAPTER III

TO STRIP AND ASSEMBLE GUN

Stripping Gun (Sequence).

CLOSE THE BREECH.

1. Remove bipod.
2. Remove cocking handle.
3. Remove trigger guard and stock.
4. Withdraw recoil spring.
5. Remove working parts (piston, breech block, firing pin).
6. Remove feed spring.
7. Remove feed piece.
8. Remove barrel.
9. Remove hand guard.
10. Unscrew and remove barrel locking nut.
11. Remove fermeture nut.

Never Strip—

1. Cartridge stop 2. Extractor 3. Back sight 4. Gas orifice screw 5. Ejector 6. Trigger mechanism	Unless absolutely necessary, or without permission of officer or sergeant.

Stripping in Detail.

CLOSE THE BREECH.

(A) Lift the feed piece to its highest extremity by pressing up as for loading, thus releasing shoulder of the piston from the feed piece to allow it to move forward slightly and rest on the sear.

(B) Pull the trigger. The cocking handle being at "R" or "A," the piston moves forward, propelled by the recoil spring. Breech now closed as when firing.

1. **Bipod.**

Unclip bipod from the clips on the hand guard, upwards turn in front of muzzle, and draw from the boss on barrel.

2. **Remove the Cocking Handle.**

(*a*) Throw the cocking handle to the left, past the vertical, and against stop.

(*b*) Draw cocking handle back about ½ inch, throw knob to the right, at an angle of 45 degrees, thus releasing C.H. from piston.

(*c*) Withdraw C.H. to the rear.

3. **Remove Trigger Guard and Stock.**

(*a*) Unscrew locking screw on left side of receiver, giving locking screw three complete turns, and so unlocking receiver from the guard stock.

(*b*) Grasp the receiver firmly with the left hand, and the stock or pistol grip with the right, push forward the stock about $\frac{3}{8}$ inch, and bring straight down, separating it from the receiver.

(*c*) The firing gear (sear, sear spring, and trigger) remain with the guard.

4. **Withdraw Recoil Spring from the inside of Piston.**

5. **Remove Recoiling Mechanism, Piston, Breech Block, and Firing Pin.**

(*a*) Insert cocking handle in the piston, the knob at an angle of 45 degrees to the right. When home, turn the knob to the vertical, to engage lugs at forward end of piston.

(*b*) Draw cocking handle to the rear, and with it the piston, breech block, and firing pin. Separate lifting B.B. from piston, tang, and reverse B.B. to allow F.P. to fall out.

6. **Remove the Feed Spring.**

(*a*) Disengage feed spring from button at top of feed piece with the forefinger of right hand, by means of hooked portion projecting to rear.

(*b*) Dismount feed spring by pushing it to the rear with the left hand, by means of the knurled button, at the same time springing it up sufficiently with the right hand to clear the pawl from the feed guides.

7. **Remove the Feed Piece.**

(*a*) Throw open feed piece cover by means of knurled knob.

(*b*) Lift leaf of rear sight.

(Both these can be done in one simultaneous action.)

(*c*) Lift feed piece to its highest position free from its slot, and turn through an angle of 180 degrees, so that the lever points to the rear. The flattened portion of the axis is now opposite the corresponding slot in the upper bearing, and the feed piece may be removed to the rear by tilting slightly rearwards.

8. **Remove the Barrel.**

(*a*) Unscrew barrel locking nut $\frac{1}{8}$ of a turn to a stop, right hand, using the dismounting wrench.

(*b*) See that left side of steel projection is in line with the guide line on the front end of receiver; this is a gauge to determine when the interrupted internal flanges of the barrel nut are disconnected with the corresponding interrupted flanges on the breech end of barrel.

(*c*) With left hand grip firmly the cylindrical portion of the receiver, and with the right grip the barrel in front of the trunnions; push straight in front, using sufficient force to disengage the barrel from B. nut.

9. **Remove the Hand Guard.**

(*a*) Turn the locking nut to the left to free its stud from engagement with the hand guard. (This stud serves to hold the hand guard in place while barrel is mounted or dismounted.)

(*b*) Remove hand guard by drawing to front.

10. **Unscrew and Remove Locking Nut.**

Upwards turn the receiver on to its rear end. Unscrew, taking note how many turns are taken to free the undercut serration of the steel projection from the serrations on the receiver. Two complete turns are usually sufficient. And care must be taken when assembling to use the same number of turns as it took to strip.

11. **Remove the Fermeture Nut.**

Incline the receiver front end downwards; the fermeture nut will slide out of receiver.

The gun is now stripped. Observe to put—the brown parts on one side (*non*-working); the bright on the other side (working), so that you can pick parts up to assemble with ease.

Assembling Gun (Sequence).

1. Fermeture nut.
2. Barrel locking nut.
3. Hand guard.
4. Barrel.
5. Feed piece.
6. Feed spring.
7. Insert piston, breech block, and firing pin.
8. Recoil spring.
9. Mount trigger guard and stock.
10. Cocking handle.
11. Bipod.

The assembling is in direct reverse to stripping.

PLATE I.—POINTS ON . MECHANISM.

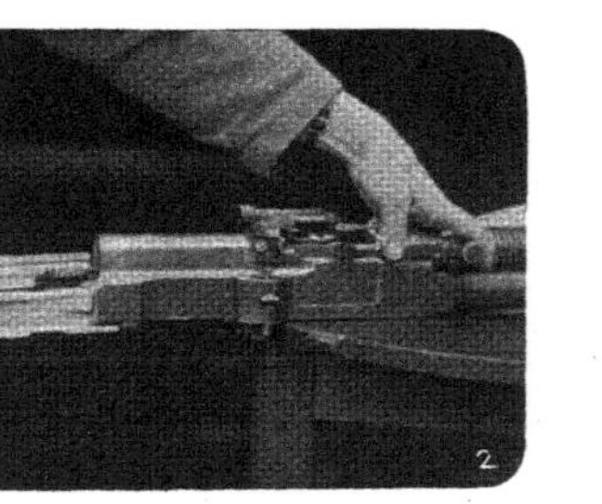

1 ASSEMBLING.
Chapter III. Page 4

2 ASSEMBLING.
Chapter III. Page 4

3 ASSEMBLING.
Chapter III. Page 4

4 STRIPPING IN ACTION.
Chapter IV. Page 4

5 STRIPPING IN ACTION.
Chapter IV Page 4

6 HOT BARREL.
Chapter IV. Page 4

To face page 42.

Assembling in Detail.

1. **Fermeture Nut.**

Insert fermeture nut, turn to the open position by passing finger of left hand in the ejection opening of receiver.

See Illustration No. 1 on Plate I., facing p. 42.

2. **Barrel Locking Nut.**

Screw on barrel locking nut, engage the threads with those on front of the receiver. The serrated teeth must engage properly with the serrated teeth on top of the receiver. Remember the number of turns in assembling, usually twice.

3. **Hand Guard.**

Fix flanges into recesses on receiver, and turn barrel locking nut, to enable stud to hold while barrel is mounted.

4. **Barrel.**

Take up the barrel, muzzle upwards turned; place into position nozzle of gas cylinder through the fore end of hand guard, the positioning stud directing. Press home until the barrel is well up to the barrel locking nut. Lay the gun horizontal, using the dismounting wrench in the left hand, in the recesses of locking nut, and tighten to the left, until the teeth under the spring projection engage in those on top of the receiver.

5. **Feed Piece.**

Open the feed piece housing cover, and lift up the leaf of radial back sight. Place the stem of feed piece in the hole at bottom of feed housing. Insert with the lever pointing to the rear, passing the flat of axis through the narrow division. Turn through an angle of 180 degrees, letting the upper arm of feed piece fall into its proper position, and in one action close the cover of feed piece housing and lower the radial back sight.

6. **Replace Feed Spring.**

Push feed spring forward to feed guide by means of the knurled knob, and engage with button at top of feed piece. With a lift up with the right hand, and a push forward with the left, the spring is replaced.

7. **Insert Piston, assembled with Breech Block and Firing Pin.**

See Illustration No. 2 on Plate I., facing p. 42.

Insert in rear of receiver, and push forward with right hand, until it comes to a stop.

(*a*) It is *imperative* that the head of the firing pin is turned completely to the left.

(*b*) That the fermeture nut is at the open position. Mechanism should slip in; *no force* is necessary or permissible.

(*c*) Press lower end of feed piece to its highest position; push forward until breech is closed.

8. **Insert Recoil Spring.**

Push forward, allowing about an inch to project to rear of receiver.

9. **Mount Guard and Stock.**

See Illustration No. 3 on Plate I., facing p. 42.

(*a*) Grasp the pistol grip with right hand, as for firing (making sure trigger mechanism is properly mounted by pulling trigger).

(*b*) Engage projecting end of the recoil spring in its seating in the wall of the guard.

(*c*) Bring guard to a position under the receiver, so that the two lugs on its head are opposite recesses in the rear of receiver, the trunnions at the front being below and in advance of the hooks at the bottom of receiver.

In order that the end of recoil spring does not foul, it may be held in place by means of the end of the cocking handle.

Raise the guard vertically, and draw to the rear until solidly seated in the receiver.

(*d*) Screw up the locking screw.

10. **Mount the Cocking Handle.**

(*a*) Insert cocking handle, knob inclined at 45 degrees to right, and push forward to a stop.

(*b*) Throw knob to the left to a stop.

(*c*) Push cocking handle forward until home, and throw down to the right at safety.

The gun is now assembled.

CHAPTER IV

STRIPPING IN ACTION

(Together with the Rapid Change of Barrel in the Field).

IN action remove the least possible number of parts, in order to get at the part required.

The following component parts may require replacing in action:

1. Extractor and spring.
2. Firing pin.
3. Recoil spring.
4. Feed spring.
5. Ejector and spring.
6. Firing gear.
7. Barrel.

STRIPPING IN ACTION.

Detail.

DEFECTIVE EXTRACTOR.

1. Close breech.
2. Remove cocking handle.
3. Remove guard and stock.
4. Withdraw recoil spring.
5. Remove piston.

Replace extractor by a spare.

See Illustration No. 4 on Plate I., facing p. 42.

(*a*) Grasp the breech block with the left hand and the hand extractor with the right. Insert the hook portion of hand extractor between the last coil of the extractor spring, compress the spring and remove it.

(*b*) Hold the breech block upwards, and the extractor will fall out.

The extractor and spring may be removed without stripping the gun.

See Illustration No. 5 on Plate I., facing p. 42.

(*a*) Insert an empty cartridge case in the ejection slot.

(*b*) Close breech gently by holding back the cocking handle on the empty case, thus giving access to extractor and spring.

(*c*) Remove the extractor and spring by means of hand extractor. Replace defective part by spare.

Relay, reload, and fire.

Broken Firing Pin.

Strip to part required. Replace, assemble, and carry on.

Broken Recoil Spring.

Strip, replace, assemble, and carry on.

Broken Feed Spring.

This can be done without stripping.

Broken Feed Piece.

No spare part.

Broken Ejector and Spring.

Right-hand side of gun, use the ejector key, remove cap, take out spring and ejector, and replace.

Broken Cartridge Stop.

Take out cartridge stop holder with dismounting wrench, unscrewing the C.S. holder, and remove the stop and spring.

Firing Gear.

To Strip Trigger Mechanism (only the sergeant should do this, or No. 1 of gun).

(*a*) Place stock between knees, the guard to the front.

(*b*) With the right hand lift the hooked arm of the trigger sufficiently to clear it entirely from the vertical arm of sear.

(*c*) With the left hand catch knurled button, which is the extremity of the sear axis, and draw to the left to remove the right-hand end from its pocket.

(*d*) Lift upwards and forwards from the guard, and separate sear with spring in guard.

PLATE II.
Use of Machine Gun on a narrow frontage. The Machine Gun, commanding road, concealed with the aid of natural cover.

PLATE III.
Use of Machine Gun on narrow frontage. View of Plate II from direction of enemy.

PLATE IV.

One method of Machine Gun coming into action. It is essential to avoid undue exposure, as the essence of Machine Gun effectiveness is surprise fire. No. 1 carries gun on his arm and leg; No. 2, Spare Barrel, Spare Parts, Wrench, and Extractor; No. 3, Ammunition; Nos. 4 and 5 are Scouts and Snipers.

PLATE V

To Change Barrel—

No. 1 on gun, with the dismounting wrench, will turn locking nut $\frac{1}{6}$ turn as far as it will go, and draw barrel out of the receiver.

No. 2 grasps firmly the barrel rest, his left arm over the gun, and both hands well up near the barrel.

No. 1 disengages barrel from receiver with a backward pull.

The spare barrel is then inserted, and the locking nut turned into the locked position.

No. 2 removes bipod from the hot barrel and places it on the cold one.

See Illustration No. 6 on Plate I., facing p. 42.

The hot barrel may be carried away by passing slot in the dismounting wrench over the stud underneath the muzzle of barrel.

CHAPTER V

MECHANISM

1. To fill a strip.
2. To load.
3. To fire.
4. To unload.

1. **To Fill a Strip (by hand).**

(*a*) Examine feed strip, three rows of clips. If defective, cartridges are not firmly held, especially if middle clips have lost their curvature. If so, discard, so that they can be put through resizing tool.

See Illustration on Plate 6, p. 28.

(*b*) Place base of cartridge against nib.

(*c*) Pull to rear.

(*d*) Push with force forward and downward between the clips of the strip.

NOTE.—Care should be taken that the rims of all cartridges bear back against their stop lugs.

2. **To Load Gun.**

(*a*) Rotate cocking handle to a stop on the left; pull back cocking handle with a quick, sharp motion (opening breech) until the hook of the lower forward arm of feed piece engages with the front of the shoulder on the right bottom flange of piston; push C.H. forward, and turn to the right, down to safety.

(*b*) Raise feed piece to its utmost extremity, and with the right hand introduce a feed strip into the guides, from right to left, cartridges side down, base of cartridges to rear, held thumb uppermost; press home until the first round in strip comes against the cartridge stop.

The gun is now loaded.

3. **To Fire.**

(*a*) With cocking lever set at Automatic ("A."), press trigger, and continue to fire as long as finger is on the trigger or until the strip is emptied.

(*b*) With the cocking handle at Repetition, or "R.," single shots only are fired; in that case, pull the trigger for each shot.

(*c*) With the cocking handle at Safety ("S.") the gun is safe.

In both cases, Automatic and Repetition, the breech remains open. If pressure on the trigger is released before strip is empty, the nose of sear rises and engages in the bent of piston, when the working parts come to the rear.

When the last round is fired and the strip passes through the feed guides, the feed spring forces down the feed piece, and hook on lower arm of feed piece engages with shoulder on right lower flange of piston holding working parts to the rear.

It is therefore necessary to release trigger and to raise feed piece before inserting the next strip.

4. **To Unload Gun.**

Breech must be open. Raise feed piece (right hand). Remove strip (left hand), close breech by pressing trigger (left hand), turn cocking handle to Safety (right hand).

The gun is now unloaded.

CHAPTER VI

MECHANISM—*Continued*

1. Action of Gases.
2. Backward Movement of Piston.
3. Feed Mechanism, Backward Movement.
4. Recoil Spring.
5. Feed Mechanism, Forward Movement.
6. Forward Movement of Piston.
7. Shock of Discharge.

Action of Gases.

(STRIP GUN.)

1. **Action of Gases when First Round is Fired.**

Suppose the shot has been fired, the gases drive the bullet forward up the bore of the barrel, and the spent gases escape through the gas vent in the barrel, through the gas nozzle ring, into the gas cylinder, where they expand according to the adjustment of the gas regulator, and out through the gas nozzle in the rear, and strike the cup-shaped forward extremity of the piston, driving the working parts to the rear and compressing the recoil spring between the bushing in the piston and its seating in the floating collar, or rear wall, or standard of the guard.

2. **Backward Movement of Piston.**

As the piston is driven backward, the *Firing Pin* is withdrawn from the face of the breech block, owing to the fact that the lug on the bottom of the firing pin is engaged in the recess on the lug on the top of the piston.

On the further backward movement, the right side of the inclined cam groove, on its upper surface, bears on the right-hand side of the lug under the *Fermeture Nut*, causing the fermeture nut to rotate clockwise to the right, and this causes the interrupted threads to disengage in the corresponding interrupted threads in the breech block, and unlocks the breech.

The lug on the top of the *Firing Pin* following the cam groove in the dome-shaped top of the receiver is rotated to the left, and engages behind the shoulder of the breech block. The piston, still moving backward, withdraws the breech block to the rear along with the *Extractor.* The claws on extractor holding the rim of the spent cartridge case withdraws it from the chamber. The *Ejector* on the right side of receiver comes in contact with the right side of the base of cartridge, throwing it to the left, through the *Ejector Opening*, into the deflector bag.

The piston now finishes its backward movement, and the recoil spring is compressed between its bushing in the piston and its seating in the rear wall of guard, ready to send piston forward.

3. **Feed Mechanism, Backward Movement.**

As the piston moves backward, the *Upper Ramp*, on the right side of piston, bears against the rear arm of feed piece, causing the upper arm to rotate from right to left. The pawl on the upper arm also moves from right to left, and, engaging in one of the centre holes in feed strip, carries it from right to left, bringing the fresh charge under the blade of the receiver and up against the cartridge stop. The charge is now in a position to be fed forward.

4. **Forward Movement (Recoil Spring).**

When the gases have expended their force and compressed the *Recoil Spring* between its seating in bushing of piston and the standard of the guard, the recoil spring now extends itself, and drives the working parts forward to their initial position, the recoil spring having a pressure of about 50 pounds.

5. **Feed Mechanism, Forward Movement.**

As the piston commences to move forward, the lower ramp, on the right side of the piston, acting on the lower front arm of the feed piece, forces feed lever to rotate from left to right. The pawl on the upper arm of lever, with its inclined shape, moves in the same direction, from left to right, and is forced over into the next space of feed strip. The feed piece is forced down by the feed spring. The pawl on the feed spring, being engaged in one of the rear holes of strip, prevents the strip from moving to the right.

6. **Forward Movement of Piston.**

As the piston moves forward in its travels it carries with it the firing pin, which is kept over to the left shoulder of the breech block by the groove in the receiver.

The firing pin, carried forward by the piston, takes with it the breech block, which bears against the *Ejector*, pressing it outwards, thus allowing the free forward movement of the working parts. In its further forward movement the top of the face of the breech block comes in contact with the bottom of the base of a fresh cartridge (which has already been loosened from the strip by the blade in the receiver), and carries it forward towards the breech, where the extractor grips the cartridge as soon as it is home in the chamber.

In the further forward movement of the piston, the lug on the top of the firing pin, travelling in the cam portion of the groove in the roof of receiver, is rotated to the right, and at the same time the left side of the cam groove on the top of piston bears against the left side of the cam lug on the fermeture nut, and rotates the fermeture nut (anti-clockwise) over to the left, thus locking the interrupted threads on the breech block with those on the fermeture nut, and locking the breech.

The piston then still travels forward, carrying with it the firing pin, which emerges through the face of the breech block, strikes the cap and explodes the charge. At the end of the forward movement the cup of piston fits over nozzle of gas cylinder.

7. **Shock of Discharge.**

The shock of discharge is taken by the rear end portion of fermeture nut bearing against its seating in receiver.

Automatic Fire.

1. To Fire First Shot.
2. To Fire Subsequent Shots.
3. To Fire Repetition or Single Shots.
4. To Cease Fire.
5. Safety.
6. Position of the Mechanism after a Strip has been Thrown Out.
7. To Feed with a Fresh Strip.

1. **To Fire the First Shot.**

Turn the cocking handle to "Auto" ("A.") regulator opposite deep recess. On pressure being applied to the trigger, the sear spring receives its first extension, and the hook on upper arm of trigger bears against step on the vertical arm of sear.

On further pressure of trigger the sear block is forced to rotate on its axis, disengaging the nose of sear from the bent on piston, allowing the recoil spring to push forward the working parts.

2. **To Fire Subsequent Shots.**

If cocking handle remains at "A.," pressure is maintained on trigger, and nose of sear remains depressed, and cannot engage in bent of piston; therefore the working parts move backward and forward until strip is exhausted.

3. **To Fire Repetition or Single Shots.**

Turn C.H. to "R."

When the trigger is pressed, the hooked arm of the trigger pulls vertical arm of sear to the rear, rotating the sear and releasing it from the bent, thus allowing the working parts to be carried forward.

As the sear is released from the bent, the tail of the trigger is depressed by the upper wall of shallow hole in the circular wall of cocking handle, thus causing the upper arm to rise and the hook to disengage itself from the vertical arm of sear. The sear spring now comes into play, rotating the sear to its highest position, and the nose of the sear engages into the bent of the piston, preventing the next forward movement.

Consequently the trigger has to be released and pressed each time a round is fired.

When the trigger is released, the sear spring pulls the trigger forward, and the hooked arm engages over the vertical arm of sear.

4. **To Cease Fire.**

When pressure on the trigger is released, the sear block rises to its highest position, and the nose of the sear engages in the bent of piston, preventing the working parts from going forward.

5. **Safety.**

If cocking handle is at " S.," the solid part of the disc is brought opposite the tail of the trigger, and cannot be drawn to the rear.

6. **Position of Mechanism after a Strip has been thrown out by the Feed Lever, or the Working Parts drawn to the Rear as before Loading.**

The two positions are identical. When the last round of a strip has been fired, the strip is thrown out, and as there is nothing to support the feed mechanism, the feed piece is forced down by the feed spring, and the forward lower arm of feed piece engages in front of the shoulder on the right bottom flange of the piston, holding the working parts to the rear. The bent is now back and clear of the sear.

7. **To Feed with a Fresh Strip.**

Push up feed piece to its fullest extent, thus freeing its forward lower arm from the shoulder on the piston. This allows the recoil spring to carry the piston forward until the bent engages with the sear.

CHAPTER VII

ADJUSTMENT OF GAS REGULATOR

IN order that the working of the gun may be regular, sufficient power must be available to ensure a complete recoil of the piston. The power may vary because of insufficient oiling, dust, or fouling in the mechanism. Again, the pressure of powder gases may vary because of temperature, deteriorated powder, or badly worn rifling.

The **Regulator** affords the means of varying the power which works the gun. Under normal conditions it should be at 25 or 2½. To test automatic action, gun in perfect condition.

(*a*) One shot only at each pull of trigger. If more than one shot is fired at a time, it shows that the piston does not recoil sufficiently to catch on sear.

(*b*) The claw of the pawl should catch in the opening in the strip at each shot. If pawl rides over top of strip, instead of catching, it shows the piston does not recoil enough to throw the feed lever through a complete stroke.

(*c*) The ejection should be regular and energetic.

If these three points are not satisfactory it may be concluded that there is a lack of power, and the regulator should be screwed up from 5 to 10 divisions.

On the other hand, *too much power* is not desirable, as the vibration due to the violent action of the mechanism necessarily affects the accuracy.

Less power required, then the gun is hot.

CHAPTER VIII

POINTS BEFORE, DURING, AND AFTER FIRING

Before Firing.

1. **Cock the Gun.**—See that the gun is properly assembled, and that no part is defective or deficient. Test mechanism by rapidly opening and closing breech and pressing the trigger.

2. See that the bore of barrel is clean, clear, and dry. Pull back cocking handle, and pass rod through bore.

3. See that gas regulators of both barrels are set at zero.

4. Oil all moving parts lightly. A moderate amount of oil (lubricating) is sufficient for this. Give all parts requiring it an oiling. It may be through the ejection opening, and by opening the feed piece cover. In this case there is no need to strip the gun.

5. See that the barrel locking nut is tight.

6. Test the action of the ejector and cartridge stop by pressing on points; they should work freely and without stiffness.

7. Before filling, examine every strip, and see that clips are not distorted or broken.

8. Most important to see that the strips are correctly filled, the cartridges pushed home, and their rims exactly in front of the nibs on the strip.

9. See that guard locking screw is properly fixed.

10. See that all spare parts and tools are in boxes; also hand extractor, dismounting wrench, and box of small parts to hand.

11. Remove oil as far as possible from the exterior of the barrel, to prevent the giving off of fumes when the barrel gets hot; this applies to spare barrel also.

During Firing.

1. Gradually open the gas regulator until just enough to get complete ejection and ability to fire single shots. If, when the cocking handle is at "R.," the gun fires more than one round for each pressure of the trigger, screw the gas regulator up, to increase the powder gas, so that the piston is forced back sufficiently to engage the sear.

2. See that the barrel locking nut remains tight.

3. Cool barrel with sponge and water if necessary.

4. Change the barrel after 500 rounds continuous rapid fire.

5. Slightly oil, if necessary, during a cessation of fire.

6. If a miss-fire occurs, allow a short interval to elapse before pulling back the cocking handle to eject defective round. If the gun is very hot, wait at least one minute, as the heat of the barrel may be sufficient to ignite the cordite within that time.

7. During a temporary cessation of fire, set cocking handle always at safety, and slightly withdraw partially expended strip in the feed guides, to avoid danger of accidental closing of the breech.

8. Replace partly used strip for full one.

9. No strips left lying about to be damaged, or to carry dirt into the mechanism. Refill all empty strips without delay.

After Firing.

1. See that the gun is unloaded.

2. See that the bore and chamber, cup of piston, and nozzle of gas cylinder are well oiled.

3. See that the recoil spring is eased.

4. Separate live rounds from empty cases.

5. On returning to quarters, strip and clean down thoroughly, paying special attention to the chamber and gas cylinder. All parts of the mechanism want carefully cleaning.

6. Examine all strips; resize if necessary.

7. Carry out any repairs, or, if necessary, take to the armourer, along with any damaged parts which have been replaced during firing from the spare parts box.

8. Enter number of rounds fired on the Gun History Book.

Gas Attack.

During gas attack it is advisable to fire occasional bursts of fire, to prevent guns from corrosion, and to create demoralization in the ranks of the enemy.

Ammunition is more seriously affected than the gun itself. Strips must therefore be kept in their boxes, and made gas tight by strips of flannelette.

PLATE VI.
Plate V as seen from direction of enemy. The gun and men are almost completely concealed.

PLATE VII.
In trench fighting the ideal is a cross-fire, the "Hornets' Nest." As above, the Machine Gun is well placed to a flank. The more complete the enfilade becomes, the less ammunition

PLATE VIII.
Infantry line occupying a position on crest of rising ground, supported by Machine Gun on the fla

PLATE IX.
View of Plate VIII from enemy's direction, showing how difficult it is to distinguish the Machin Gun—on the extreme left—from the rest of the line.

CHAPTER IX

MECHANICAL SAFETY DEVICES

1. BREECH is closed before round is fired.

2. Owing to gas vent being half-way up the barrel, the bullet leaves the muzzle before breech is open.

3. There is never a live round in the chamber.

4. When gun is at "S." (Safety), and a partly used strip remains in the gun, it is prudent to withdraw strip to the right, after pressing up feed piece, as no cartridge then remains opposite the chamber if the breech is accidentally closed.

To resume fire, put cocking handle to "A." or "R.," and push strip to left; bring next round into the firing position.

CHAPTER X

EXAMINATION OF GUN

ANY signs of wear should be at once reported to the armourer.

1. Barrel for rust or fouling.

2. (*a*) Gas cylinder
(*b*) Piston cup
(*c*) Firing pin
(*d*) Gas regulator
} for carbon deposits.

3. (*a*) Extractor
(*b*) Cartridge stop
} for roughness.

4. (*a*) Cam on fermeture nut
(*b*) " firing pin
(*c*) " groove of receiver
(*d*) " projections on shank of cocking handle
} for burring.

Examination of Gun (in Detail).

The following are the most important points to which attention must be paid in examining the gun. Great care and attention is necessary to maintain the gun in perfect condition.

Replacements can be made of any damaged part from the spare parts always provided. Repairs and tests by means of gauges will be left to the qualified armourer.

1. **Barrel.**

See that rifling—bullet lead, chamber, and the bore—are in good condition; rear face of barrel not damaged, paying special care to the key and projections; that the stud for the barrel rest, stop for locking nut, and radiating flanges, are not damaged, and are free from dirt and rust; that the gas cylinder is clear, and will easily screw up by hand, but not so freely that it moves when carrying. See that the nozzle of the cylinder is free.

2. **Barrel Locking Nut.**

See that serrations hold properly on spring arm, threads are not damaged, and interrupted threads engage with barrel properly.

3. **Receiver.**

See that cartridge stop and ejector are working without stiffness and springs elastic; **V**- shaped cam groove for the firing pin in the rear portion is clear and smooth; that there is no obstruction in the grooves of the feed guide; that the back sight and slide are not damaged, work freely, and can be retained in any position. Examine thread for the locking nut, and see that the hand guard fits correctly.

4. **Fermeture Nut.**

See that it is not burred or cracked, and that its thread and boss are not damaged.

5. **Guard and Stock.**

See that the trigger mechanism is in good condition and works correctly; that it seats properly in the receiver; spring of sear works properly; that the collar against which the recoil spring rests is correct; that the butt is not cracked or broken; that the hinged strap is in good condition.

6. **Cocking Handle.**

See that stem is not bent; recesses on disc not deformed; and that lugs and lever are right.

7. **Firing Pin.**

See that point is not damaged; that the lower and upper bosses have their surfaces smooth.

8. **Recoil Spring.**

See that it is not cracked or broken.

9. **Breech Block.**

See that all surfaces are smooth and not burred; interrupted threads in good condition; front shoulder on the left, that the firing pin rests against, not cracked or broken; that the hole in the face, at the front, for the point of firing pin is without any obstruction.

10. **Piston Rod.**

See that all the working surfaces and cams are smooth and not burred; cup of piston not cracked; and that the bent underneath, in which the sear engages, is in order.

NOTE.—Where burrs or roughness on working parts are found during examination, the parts should be taken to the armourer, who will smooth them down with fine emery cloth. No one in any machine gun section should do this; leave it to a qualified armourer.

CHAPTER XI

CARE AND CLEANING

THE gun requires as much or more care than the service rifle. It must be kept clean and free from rust, and all parts lightly oiled. No gritty substances or emery should be used. Too much oil causes sluggish working and possibly a miss-fire.

Mineral oil paraffin is a convenient means of removing rust, but assists the formation of rust; so after use let it be carefully removed and the gun parts oiled with a good lubricating oil.

The corporal, No. 1 on the gun, is responsible for cleaning, and must see the gun is kept in perfect condition, ready for action.

The gun ought to be cleaned daily for ten days after firing, at the discretion of the officer or sergeant in charge of the section.

1. **To Clean the Barrel.**

Fouling can be easily removed before it has time to become hard; the barrel, therefore, should be cleaned as soon after firing as possible. Boiling water method is recommended from breech to nozzle of barrel. Use several pints of boiling water; this extracts the cordite gases forced into the metal by the force of explosion. But great care must be exercised to see that all water is removed from barrel and from the gas cylinder. Remember the barrel is expensive and difficult to replace, and above all pay special care to the chamber.

In box of small parts you will find reflector mirror; look down breech when the gun is assembled, or you may use it through the ejector opening.

Use cleaning rod and 4 by 2 strip until clean; then leave a film of oil in the bore by using a slightly oiled strip.

The double pull-through with wire gauze is only used for hard fouling or rust, and then the wire gauze must be well oiled before using. The best method is to fix the barrel in a vice, or let it be held by a man, while one man works either end of the pull-through. Never use, as a rule, the pull-through more than *three times*, to avoid wearing the barrel, when the wire gauze is on. Afterwards put it on one side and use dry flannelette till the bore is rag-clean. Finally, a slightly oiled strip to leave a film of oil.

Remember, the utmost care must be taken to avoid allowing the cord to rub against muzzle or breech, to avoid a groove being worn by the cord. If this happens at the chamber end, it will tend to burst cartridge cases; and if at the muzzle end, will destroy the accuracy of the barrel.

2. **Gas Cylinder.**

This must be cleaned out to remove fouling, and to allow the gas regulator to be turned by hand, without using the dismounting wrench.

Gas cylinder must be dry and all traces of water removed. Until all water is out, the gas pressure may be insufficient to ensure automatic action.

Gas piston wipe with flannel, and if bad soak in oil and use screwdriver.

Take special care of annular rings, and this would allow escape of gas if not correct.

3. **Recoil Spring.**

When gun is not in use the breech should always be kept closed, so as to avoid fatiguing the recoil spring.

4. **Cup of Piston.**

Look for fouling, and remove, if any, with an oily piece of flannelette, leaving the cup slightly oiled, unless gun is to be fired immediately.

5. **Firing Pin.**

Look for fouling, and remove.

6. All parts must be thoroughly cleaned with a mixture of equal parts of oil (lubricating and mineral). Afterwards dried, and lightly oiled with lubricating only, before parts are replaced.

Watch for dirt and remove from all stationary portions; look at recesses likely to harbour dirt. Remove dried oil by the use of turpentine.

After all parts have been replaced, rub exterior over with a piece of flannelette, lightly oiled with lubricating oil.

7. Any signs of wear to be attended to by armourer.

During Gas Attack.—By use of blankets soaked in anti-gas solution, protect your gun and ammunition.

Ammunition boxes must be made gas-tight by strips of flannelette.

After a Gas Attack.—Clean and re-oil guns immediately, and as soon as possible strip and clean with boiling water and soda.

8. Finally, "use common sense."

CHAPTER XII

IMMEDIATE ACTION ("I.A.") AND STOPPAGES

WHEN a failure occurs always use "I.A." (Immediate Action) as follows:

1. Open breech by pulling back cocking handle, and examine ejection opening.

2. Remove jammed round with the hand extractor, or cleaning rod, if necessary, and see that the chamber is clear.

3. Withdraw strip if a remedy is to be applied; otherwise push it forward, bringing the next round into the loading position.

4. If the gun cannot be cocked—

   (*a*) No. 1 on the gun will pull on to cocking handle, while at the same time No. 2 withdraws the strip, using in this case the necessary force.

   (*b*) Reload with a fresh strip and go on firing.

CHAPTER XIII

STOPPAGES: THEIR CAUSE AND REMEDY, BY APPLICATION OF "I.A."

No. 1.—Jam on First Round.

Failure.	*Result.*	*Cause.*	*Remedy.*
Jam on first round of strip.	Bad introduction.	Strip not properly home before pressing trigger.	"I.A."

No. 2.—Miss-Fires.

Failure.	*Result.*	*Cause.*	*Remedy.*
Miss-fires.	(*a*) Breech closed.	Defective ammunition.	"I.A.," and examine ejection opening for position of working parts.
If again.	(*b*) Breech closed.	Locking nut not screwed up (loose).	"I.A." and screw up.
"	(*c*) Breech closed; round not exploded.	Broken firing pin.	"I.A." Note round ejected, and if not exploded.

MISS-FIRES—*continued.*

Failure.	*Result.*	*Cause.*	*Remedy.*
If again.	(*d*) Breech closed (*partly*).	Broken or weak recoil spring.	"I.A." and replace.
"	(*e*) Breech block home, but not *fully locked.*	Loose cap or brass filings, or dirt on breech block or fermeture nut.	"I.A." Dismount and remove dirt or obstruction.

NO. 3.—FAULTS IN FEED.

Failure.	*Result.*	*Cause.*	*Remedy.*
Faults in feed.	Bad introduction.	(*a*) Loose round in strip.	"I.A." Change strip, and resize before using again.
"	Live round on empty case.	(*b*) Lack of gas pressure or excessive friction.	Screw up the gas regulator ½ to 1 division, or clean.
"		(*c*) Damaged strip.	"I.A." (No. 4). No. 1 pulls on C.H., and No. 2 removes the strip and feeds with a new strip.

No. 4.—Breakages.

Failure.	*Result.*	*Cause.*	*Remedy.*
Breakages.	Breech only partly closed and live round against empty case in chamber.	(*a*) Broken extractor or spring.	"I.A.," and replace. If extractor in good condition, screw gas regulator further home.
,,	Breech block jam, and a live cartridge or an empty case in feed way.	(*b*) Broken ejector or spring.	"I.A.," and replace.

CHAPTER XIV

SPARE PARTS AND TOOLS

THE following spare parts and tools are issued with each gun:

Barrel	1
Box (tin) containing small parts... ...	1
Brush (cleaning) for gas cylinder ...	1
Brushes (wire)	2
Can (oil)	1
Cleaner (gas cylinder)	1
Covers for foresight	1
Ejector	1
Extractor (hand)	2
Gauzes (wire)	2
Hammer	1
Key (ejector)	1
Pin (firing)...	2
Pull-through (double)	2
Punch (No. 3 M.G.)	1
Reflector mirror	1
Rod, cleaning bore, with brass connection slotted for flannelette	1
Screwdriver (large)	1
Screw (locking)	2
Sights (front)	1

Spring, cartridge stop	1
„ ejector	1
„ extractor	2
„ feed	2
„ recoil	1
„ sear	2
Tool for resizing strips	1
Wrench (dismounting)	2

One gun limber for each gun, top part detachable, fitted for ammunition boxes, spare parts box, and for the gun and spare barrel.

Also hopper, or strip filling machine.

The box provided for spare parts is of the same dimensions as that for strips; it has a hinged lid, and is secured by a spring catch. Fittings are provided to take all the spare parts and tools, and the box has a leather handle for carrying purposes.

A bag should be provided as a satchel with shoulder strap, and used for emergency parts. Box empty weighs $6\frac{1}{2}$ pounds; filled, $12\frac{1}{4}$ pounds.

CHAPTER XV

GUN DRILL FOR THE HOTCHKISS PORTABLE MACHINE GUN

IT is important to note that the drill and general tactical principles laid down as governing the use of machine guns are identical for every class of this weapon.

Gun drill is a most important feature in the training of a section; it teaches discipline and steadiness, and must be carried out at the double; therefore smartness and accuracy must be the aim of all machine gun sections. Without these qualities the gun drill of a section has very little value.

It must be remembered that the machine gun is always a weapon of opportunity, particularly adapted for surprise effect. Therefore, aim at quick movement, and select men who are enthusiastic about their work, and possessing the following qualifications: good physique, good eyesight, calm temperament, fair education, and mechanical aptitude. Some part of every attendance should include machine gun drill, until all connected with machine guns should be so familiar with the gun that it should come as second

PLATE X.
Machine Gun in action, hidden by fold in the ground.

PLATE XI.
The Machine Gun Section is seen in action. Nos. 1 and 2 with the Gun. The Gun is ready to fire, so No. 2 holds up his hand over No. 1. Scouts, on either side, guard the Gun from surprise attack and also select next position forward. No. 3 acts as connecting [illegible] from Gun [illegible]

PLATE XII.

PLATE XIII.

Plates XII and XIII depict Machine Gun Section advancing as part of Infantry Line. Easily mistaken as Infantry Line even at close range.

To face page 81.

nature in both drill and "proper handling" of the gun.

Machine Gun Drill.

MEN OF SECTION.

No. 1, corporal, is the firer. He will personally clean and look after his gun, and ensure that the mechanism is working smoothly.

On going into action, or receiving any command in gun drill, he repeats all orders. He observes his own fire, and makes all the necessary alterations in range and direction.

No. 2 assists No. 1 at the gun; carries the spare barrel and ammunition boxes; attends to the feeding of the gun; watches for signals from the M.G. sergeant or officer, and generally assists No. 1, taking his place if casualty.

No. 3 is ammunition carrier, and takes position about five paces in the rear of gun.

No. 4 lies near the limber, ready to carry more ammunition to No. 3 when he signals for further supplies.

No. 5 acts as scout, range-finder, or sniper, to protect the gun.

Exchange of duties should be frequently carried out; for this reason "Change Rounds" in drill is given.

It is important to note that all working the gun keep perfectly still until command "Easy" is given.

A man lying still is difficult to see; any movement gives the position away.

"Fall In."

On the command "Fall In," gun detachments fall in 5 paces in front of their respective guns.

Command—"Number."

The team is numbered from the right.

Command—"Change Rounds."

No. 1 repeats order, turns to right, and doubles round to left of detachment, which simultaneously re-numbers. (This is to remind section that every man must be able to do another's work in case of casualty.)

Command—"Take Post."

The gun detachment turns smartly to the right and doubles round in rear of gun. No. 1 takes his position and lies on the left of his gun.

No. 2 lies on left of spare barrel and ammunition box.

Nos. 3, 4, and 5 lie down ready for their work, or to take place of "casualties," when "Change Round" is given.

For drill—Target 25 yards from gun.

Instructor will then point out a spot, not more than 5 yards away, in front of guns, indicating the spot guns are to be mounted.

Three aiming marks are given on the target.

Points Instructor and Gunners must Observe:—

(*a*) Regulator set correctly, the same for spare barrel as gun.
(*b*) Barrel rests clamped.
(*c*) Radial back sight at normal.
(*d*) Breech closed.
(*e*) Foresight protector removed.
(*f*) Shoulder straps down.

No. 1 must always have on him—

(*a*) Dismounting wrench.
(*b*) Hand extractor.
(*c*) Box of small parts.

These may be carried by No. 2 and handed to No. 1 when ready.

No. 2 looks for following:

(*a*) Regulator of spare barrel as on gun.
(*b*) Look to see rounds are properly on strip, and strips correctly in boxes.

Warning—"Stand by to Mount Gun."

Command—"Mount Gun."

No. 1 repeats order; sets barrel rest; picks up gun by the small of stock (right hand), and left hand round legs of barrel rest; doubles forward with the gun; places it in position in reference to the targets, bipod firmly on the ground; raises the shoulder strap, and places the dismounting wrench, hand extractor, and box of small parts conveniently near.

No. 2 doubles up with the ammunition box, spare barrel, and box of spares, placing the barrel and ammunition box in a good position to feed gun, opening the ammunition box in readiness.

Points to Note:—

(*a*) No. 1: Barrel rest properly set, and leaning slightly forward.
(*b*) Gun mounted in reference to target.
(*c*) Good position behind gun, with shoulder strap raised.

No. 2 of gun must be in a good position, close to No. 1. Box and spare barrel conveniently near for use, barrel under gun. And, *most important*, no movement of any of the section when once down in their prone position.

Warning—"Stand by to Load Gun."

Command—"Load" (4 seconds).

No. 1 cocks the gun and raises feed piece.

No. 2 inserts the strip, until first round comes against the cartridge stop.

Points to Note:—

(*a*) Gun correctly loaded.
(*b*) Done cleanly.
(*c*) Cocking handle at "R."

Sight Setting and Laying.

Commands—

"Range."
"Target."
"Auto." or "Rep."

Orders—

The range should be given, then some outstanding feature in the landscape or on the target, and lastly the actual objective.

Example: "Range 500; right hand group of figures; right hand figure."

No. 1 will then fix rear sight to range given, and lay his gun on the object (repeating all orders as given), and when ready to fire calls "Up."

No. 2 with his hand over No. 1 and eyes on the commander.

At given signal to fire No. 2 taps No. 1 on shoulder, who then opens fire as previously ordered.

Points to Notice:—

See that all orders are carried out correctly.

Examine back-sight (correct range), position of gun on target, cocking handle. Note C.H. always at "R." unless "A." is given.

And the method of three objects, right, centre, and left, practised.

Warning—"Stand by to Unload Gun."

Command—"Unload Gun."

No. 1 sees gun is cocked, and lifts feed piece.

No. 2 withdraws feed piece.

No. 1 presses trigger, lowers back sight to zero, and closes the shoulder strap.

No. 2 picks up ammunition and spare boxes and barrel.

No. 1 calls out, "Gun clear."

Command—" Dismount Gun."

Warning—"Stand by to Dismount Gun"; then, "Dismount gun."

No. 1 picks up gun and doubles back to former position.

No. 2 follows with barrel and boxes.

No. 1 closes up barrel rest, and lays gun on its *right side*, to show breech closed.

FOR PRACTICE AT THIS STAGE.

Command—" Change Rounds."

As in gun drill and "Action"—

No. 1 falls out.
No. 2 takes No. 1's place.
No. 3 takes No. 2's place.
No. 4 takes No. 3's place.
Directly they are down they renumber off, and carry on as in "Take Post."

Command—" Action."

Warning—"Stand by for Action."

ORDER—"ACTION."

Same as "Mount Gun," only No. 1 is given the range, nature of fire, and plan of action or object first—all of which he repeats. Adjusts regulator, and doubles up into immediate action, selecting the best position for the object given.

Examine to see following points:

1. Sight set correctly as ordered.
2. Target—good position taken.
3. Regulators of both barrels alike.
4. Barrel well forward on bipod.

Command—" Out of Action."

Warning—Stand by for "Out of Action."

"OUT OF ACTION."

This is same as "Dismount Gun," and means "Cease Fire." Unload, dismounting gun and retiring at the double to former position.

"Change Barrel" can be always taken in this drill as the barrel must be changed in action after 600 rounds of continuous firing (particulars given in Chapter IV.).

CHAPTER XVI

TIME-LIMIT TESTS

1.	Mount gun	10	seconds.
2.	Load	4	„
3.	Sight setting and laying	5	„
4.	Unload	3	„
5.	Dismount gun	8	„
6.	Action	15	„
7.	Out of action	15	„
8.	Changing barrel ...	15	„
9.	Stripping gun	35	„
10.	Assembling gun ...	75	„
11.	Changing firing pin ...	30	„
12.	Changing extractor ...	15	„
13.	Firer alone	250	„
14.	Firer and aid loading ...	400	„

CHAPTER XVII

SIGNALS FOR CONTROL AND OBSERVATION OF FIRE

SIGNALS are used exactly the same for all machine guns of various types. At no time more than during this war of machinery has this been more keenly recognized. The noise is so tremendous that shouted orders are hard, if not impossible, to hear. Consequently, machine gun sections must be frequently practised in M.G. signals and semaphore, so that communications can be correctly carried out, and on all occasions when guns are firing or drill the following signals should be used in controlling fire:

Command.	*Signal.*	*By Whom Given.*
"Action."	Both arms raised from the sides to a position in line with the shoulders. Repeat until seen and complied with.	Controlling Officer.
"Out of Action."	Arms swing in circular motion in front of body, shoulder high.	Do.
"Ready to Fire."	Holding hand up.	No. 2 of gun section.
"Prepare to Fire."	Hand up.	Controlling Officer.
"Open Fire."	Hand dropped.	Do.
"Cease Fire."	Elbow close to side, hand moved backwards and forwards horizontally in front of body.	Do.

SEMAPHORE ALPHABET AND NUMERAL SIGNS

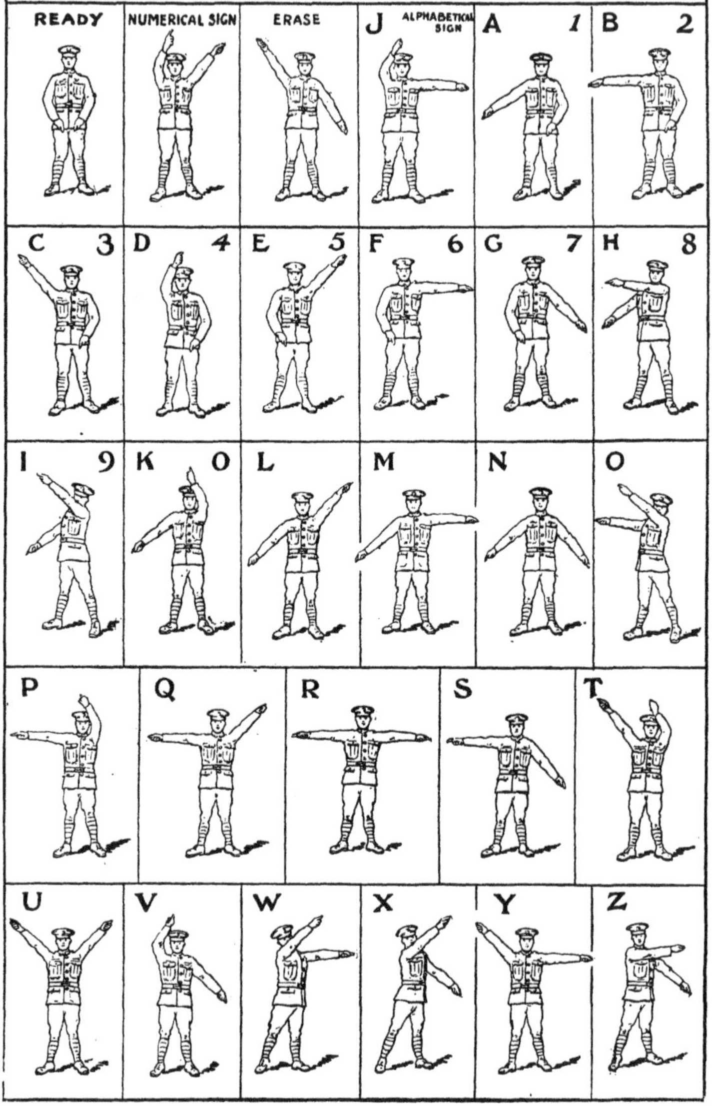

READY	NUMERICAL SIGN	ERASE	J ALPHABETICAL SIGN	A 1	B 2
C 3	D 4	E 5	F 6	G 7	H 8
I 9	K 0	L	M	N	O
P	Q	R	S	T	
U	V	W	X	Y	Z

Signals.

In semaphore for observation of fire, it will generally be necessary for observers to signal results from a flank, and the following semaphore code is used.

In the Hotchkiss machine gun letters have recently been changed from the other gun signals.

A.	More ammunition required.
O.	Plus—meaning fire observed at least 50 yards over the target.
S.	Minus—meaning fire observed at least 50 yards short of the target.
K.	Range correct.
R.	Meaning fire observed to right of target.
L.	Meaning fire observed to left of target
W.	Unobserved—meaning no observation obtained.
R.	Range—meaning range correct.

The signaller at the observation post should give the "Call Up" to show that the observers are ready. "O" and "S" may be repeated for multiples of 50 yards. Thus, "OO" would mean "Fire observed at least 100 yards over the target," and "SSS" "Fire observed at least 150 yards short of the target."

Signals should be repeated from the gun position if this can be done without disclosing the position to the enemy.

Let semaphore be taught to all M.G. sections, as much by hands as with flags.

In addition to the semaphore signals, it is advisable to have some simple CODE OF SIGNALS, known to the Hotchkiss gunners of the battalion. This can be arranged by the M.G. officer. The following may be suggested :—

A full strip of ammunition showing bright brass of the cartridges turned in the direction in which one wants to send the message. The man sending the message must be in the prone position, so that movements are unobserved by the enemy.

1. "Send up more ammunition."

Signal: One full strip moved up and down vertically.

2. "Reinforce," implying casualty; and in this case assistance should always be by *two* men, not *one* man.

Signal: One full strip moved horizontally or laterally.

3. "Ready," gun being ready for action. This is very necessary where a gun is forward to give covering fire, as in the "platoon in the offensive," when concerted action is required.

Signal: Two full strips—one in each hand—moved horizontally or laterally.

4. "Gun out of action," implying unable to fire through being damaged.

Signal: Two full strips moved up and down vertically.

Observe that when the Hotchkiss machine gun is in action, only two, or possibly three, of the section are with the gun, the remainder being in the rear with ammunition; consequently the signals will be from the gun to the other members of the machine gun section.

As a signal of "acknowledgment" they can repeat all signals sent.

Important.—The two signals "Ready" and "Gun out of action" must in every case be sent back to the platoon commander by the senior gunner who receives it. This is especially necessary with the "platoon in the offensive."

CHAPTER XVIII

RANGE CHART: OFFENSIVE

BEFORE any advance is made the range chart should be made by range-taker.

The range-taker chooses likely positions for machine guns, under cover, in the line of attack, and finds the range.

This he writes opposite to them in right-hand margin. Having taken ranges, he calculates from range to the objective, and writes on the left-hand margin and crosses out ranges on the right.

Section commanders, on reaching any point during the advance, can immediately read off his range from objective point by glancing at the left-hand margin.

In this Range Chart the ranges are taken from the gun position and on the left-hand side margin and purposely crossed off.

Then as you advance with gun you read from the left-hand margin as in the original sheet with this note.

Offensive Range Chart

RANGE CARD (KEY RANGE E)
for an attack on Enemy's position at Leamington, from a point on Golf Links.

0	First OBJECTIVE	950
150	BLACK HUT	800
350	GATE IN HEDGE	600
500	HAYSTACKS	450
650	GREEN BUSHES	300
700	CLUMP OF TREES	250
950	POINT ON LINKS	0

DIRECTION OF ATTACK
N.N.W.

5th July, 1918 11 a.m. F. W. BULL,
M.G. Sergt., 2nd W.V.R.

Specimen Range Card for Defence.

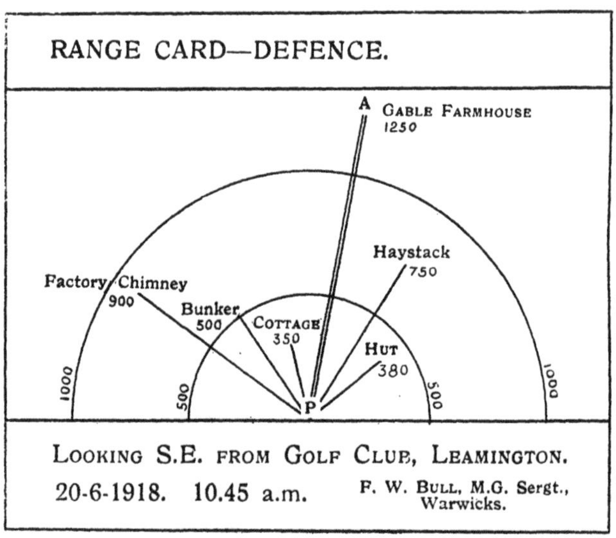

In this chart the line P A is a sighting line, from which all other points whose ranges are to be found are sighted. A double line should always be drawn.

For both offensive and defensive work a machine gun section should always have an escort.

PLATE XIV.

Machine Gun in defence. The main object must be to create a cross-fire to cover the whole of advancing enemy, or to fall on the enemy's front line parapet.

PLATE XV.

PLATE XVI.
Machine Gun Section with Limber, containing Machine Gun, Accessories, and Boxes of Ammunition.

PLATE XVII.
Hotchkiss Machine Gun Section, with Limber, containing Gun, Spare Barrel and Parts, and

DESCRIPTION AND CONTENTS OF HOTCHKISS GUN CART.

The cart is similar in design to the Lewis Machine Gun Cart, consisting of a box on a steel-framed under-carriage, with draught handle, mounted on an axletree with two bicycle wheels with flat, solid rubber tyres.

At each corner are props underneath, so that the cart can be maintained in the horizontal position when necessary. The props are lowered, or raised, and held by a spring plunger.

The draught handle is of tubular steel, and can be fixed to either end of cart, and when not in use is fixed under the cart by a spring clip and two leather straps attached to the frame.

At each corner of the cart is a loop for the fixing of a drag rope.

The lid is covered with canvas, attached by hinges to the side, sloping from the middle.

It is so arranged to prevent water from entering when the lid is closed. A spring catch secures lid in closed position. On the top are two pairs of straps for securing the drag ropes.

Contents.

Cart, with drag ropes.
Gun, assembled.
Barrel, spare.
1 Box, spare parts and tools.
1 Box, machine filling, for feed strips.
8 Boxes, feed strips ammunition, each containing 10 feed strips (filled), each with 30 rounds of ammunition—total, 2,400 rounds.
Wallet, leather, with tools for cart.
Total weight of cart, filled (approx.), 5 cwt.

CHAPTER XIX

CHARACTERISTICS AND TACTICS OF MACHINE GUNS

(From Notes made at Lectures given at Hayling Island School of Gunnery.)

It will prove of great interest to have some idea of the working of machine guns during this Great War, and for this reason the author introduces this lecture before going into the details of the Hotchkiss gun, to enable those who study it to start their course with interest and enthusiasm.

The tactics of the machine guns in open or trench warfare are the same; this applies to (1) Advance Guards; (2) Rear Guards; (3) Outposts. The machine gun in battle is extremely valuable; one cannot emphasize this sufficiently.

The Germans made this discovery long ago, and have made good use of it. Their machine gunners are experts, and they consider each gun worth fifty or more men.

In their retirement from within striking distance of Paris in 1914 they used few infantry, but plenty of artillery and machine guns. Consequently, they held up the British advance all day with well-selected positions; this can be easily understood, and teaches this lesson—*economize your infantry*—as it is the infantry who will eventually end the show.

The Germans in their *retreats* always realize this, and as their infantry falls back it is behind their machine guns and artillery.

In doing this they have always collected stragglers, the "halt, lame, and blind," with instructions for rear guard that these men must surrender, and so delay the advance.

The Vickers is the gun of the Machine Gun Corps. It is heavy—maximum weight 86 pounds with water jacket filled. As the lecture proceeds we will call it the "heavy machine gun," and without doubt the finest heavy machine gun in the world; but being heavy, it is not so mobile as the light Hotchkiss or Lewis guns used by the infantry. Therefore, the heavy machine guns are the guns of the Machine Gun Corps, and the lighter guns our infantry weapon.

In a battalion in France you have 16 light guns, 4 to a company, and 1 to each platoon. And in support, under the control of the brigade machine gun officer, the heavy Vickers guns.

Characteristics to Remember.

1. Obviously, the light machine guns go with the advance guard in the first wave.

2. And the heavy (Vickers) with the main guard for defence.

You get, therefore, co-operation between the heavy and light guns.

In the falling back, the first to retire is the infantry, covered by the light machine guns; then the heavy machine guns move to selected positions to hold up the attack, waiting the light guns to stand fast, and if necessary to sacrifice themselves and gunners.

The heavy guns now bring an overhead cross fire to bear on the advancing enemy, and if possible hold up the advance, to allow the main body to get away.

Infantry, engineers, and transports, the heavies cover all this. Therefore increase, if the Brigadier can, your machine gun fire—the more the better; you cannot over-estimate its value. They can use overhead fire. Supposing our trenches were on one side of the valley, and the enemy's on the opposite hill, overhead fire could be used to advantage, as the Vickers can use their elevating wheel, and so create a "curtain of fire."

By now the light guns have moved back, and you notice now their chief characteristic (mobility); and they can now move under the protection of the heavy guns, and are able to co-operate in the general defence of the combined machine gun fire.

Now notice some of the advantages of the light guns:

1. They can defend stretches of open ground, and so relieve the infantry.

2. Owing to bursts of fire, they can be used in defiles and streets, or to guard roads.

3. They can be laid on a gap in a hedge or wall by which enemy must pass, and so prevent their passage.

4. They can be used to surprise the oncoming enemy; the use of machine guns for surprise cannot be too strongly emphasized.

5. Let the enemy advance unsuspectingly, and when in the middle of an open space bring a withering fire (automatic) to bear upon them.

6. Always remember the importance of cross fire—guns on the flanks, the "hornets' nest."

7. When guns are not used in trenches, they should, when possible, be placed to bring oblique or enfilading fire on—

(*a*) The enemy's trenches.

(*b*) The ground over which the enemy must pass in his attack.

(*c*) Our own front line trenches in case enemy penetrates them.

In all cases the gun should be, if possible, covered from fire from the front, and should be able to sweep the front of the entrenched line with cross fire.

Thus, although each gun may be firing to its flank, its front is swept by the fire of a neighbouring gun. Nothing can live in such a hail of bullets, and it is called the "hornets' nest."

In passing we will consider the machine guns used by cavalry. This is the Hotchkiss gun, and we will therefore deal with the Hotchkiss as a cavalry gun, its characteristic as a cavalry weapon.

1. Its mobility and heavy volume of fire, brought to bear on a small frontage, render the machine gun suitable to support a cavalry charge.

2. It can be adapted for close co-operation with a dismounted attack.

3. Its mobility and fire power render it suitable for unexpected and critical situations.

4. Greatest value when employed on a flank of the dismounted cavalry.

In dismounted action—

(*a*) Machine guns deny a position to the enemy.
(*b*) Delay the enemy's advance.

Remember, in a long-sustained action, great expenditure of ammunition, so keep guns as a reserve of fire.

In pursuit, endeavour to make the enemy's retirement into a rout.

In retirement, delay the enemy by bringing fire to bear on roads, defiles, and open spaces, thus forcing him to deploy.

Most important, use the guns in delaying any effort to turn the flanks of the rearguard.

Coming back to the infantry. Remember, the advance guards being mobile, it can concentrate on any given spot, such as bridges and roads, and for outpost work machine guns are most essential.

At the beginning of this Great War, in our retirement at Mons, it was most necessary to cover the main forces with all our few machine guns.

We had the bravest and best army in the world, under Field-Marshal Lord French—"The contemptible little army," who took the spears of Prussia to their breasts and perished, but in perishing saved Europe.

> "The little mighty force that stood for England,
> That, with their bodies for a living shield,
> Guarded her slow awaking; that defied
> The sudden challenge of tremendous odds,
> And fought the rushing legions to a stand.
> Then, stark in grim endurance, held the line.
> O little force that in your agony
> Stood fast while England girt her armour on,
> Held high our honour in your wounded hands,
> Carried our honour safe with bleeding feet,
> We have no glory great enough for you;
> The very soul of Britain keeps your day!
> O mighty little force, your way is ours,
> The land inviolate your monument."

No, "We have no glory great enough" for that old regular army which battled so stubbornly against tremendous odds at Mons and Le Cateau, on the Aisne, and later at Ypres. They saved the national honour in the acutest crisis of history, and practically ceased to exist in the doing of it.

Outnumbered, outgunned, outflanked, and in danger of destruction, all fought worthy of their great traditions, and, as Newbolt says, "Nothing but the overwhelming weight of their artillery fire saved the Germans from total repulse."

They only succeeded when the machine gun teams had been wiped out time after time, and when one by one the guns themselves had at last been blown to pieces; and in the great fight the machine gunners, by their splendid endurance, inflicted almost unimaginable loss upon the enemy.

For Outpost Work, most Essential.

We can observe many lessons from the War—one, almost the main thing, is to *economize infantry* by giving them as much rest as you can.

Think of our men all day fighting and digging; all night on the watch, waiting for sudden surprises, and when the battle comes, "like a thief in the night," you have weary troops at your disposal. So economize your men, and this is where your machine guns turn out "trumps." They can watch roads, especially at night, look out for sudden attack and surprises, and so save the infantry, letting them sleep and rest, and so able to answer the call for all emergencies.

Think of the night—lonely and dark—no knowledge of the locality, not even a friendly star. And as the weary men sleep, the machine gun section keeps vigil on its outpost work.

The enemy may advance along a road. Here, again, I emphasize—Watch all roads, and remember one Hotchkiss gun is equal to a company in this special work. On the one hand, long lines in extended order; on the other, your machine gun directly on the spot, and nothing in flesh and blood can advance with guns firing at the rate of 600 a minute. Therefore, for outpost work, invaluable.

To Defend Trenches.

By belts of cross fire, it makes it almost impossible to take the trench; the advancing line of the enemy will disappear, and unless your guns are knocked out, your position is impregnable. This is what is called by our men a "German hornets' nest"; therefore, to break them down we have introduced the tanks.

Consider the very latest way machine guns are now employed.

In the trenches very few, if any, *heavy* Vickers guns are found in the front line. They are heavy, and cannot be moved with ease, and so are likely to be captured, with plenty of ammunition.

Therefore, they build for Vickers guns concrete emplacements in the rear, and make this rear position a fortified area. In a bombardment light machine guns go to deep dug-outs, and when the bombardment lifts, and the first wave is coming, the light machine guns commence their work, and the infantry come up their communication trench to support.

One special job of the light machine guns is to look after any area not swept by the heavy Vickers guns. Therefore, you have co-operation of heavy and light guns.

Consider differences—

Light guns better at night.

Heavy guns are clumsy; therefore, to advance or retire at night, not so desirable.

Heavy gun—weapon of position; don't fire too often, or it will be knocked out by artillery.

Light Guns.—They can fire and change position rapidly, and therefore, for front line work, use the light gun.

In night attacks know how to employ guns.

Consider our attacking the Hun lines. You must in this case use the light machine guns to break down the machine gun fire of the enemy, by *bursts* of fire. Our artillery barrage goes on ahead of our advance, but this in itself cannot keep down the hostile machine gun fire of the Huns, so we have to supplement the artillery fire by our own machine gun fire.

You can have your light guns in the firing-line, and behind the line, in reserve, the heavy guns, watching communicating trenches for enfilading fire, and also to prevent the enemy getting into their trenches for support.

To further this end you push out at night before they attack your guns. Remember, with the light guns you cannot sustain your traversing fire easily; therefore your chief job is to watch for enemy machine guns, and play on them automatic, direct, concentrated fire.

The light guns can never take on the heavy guns; you might just as well put up a destroyer to fight a battleship. If the light guns take on the heavy guns they will get knocked out when the infantry does advance. The light guns therefore wait, and come up (1) to consolidate the new position; (2) to help the infantry to gain superiority at the decisive point; (3) to reach the captured position as soon as possible, in order to pursue the enemy with fire, and to allow their own infantry to re-form in companies and platoons; (4) and to watch for and repel counter-attacks.

The battle is now over.

PLATE XVIII.—PLATOON IN THE OFFENSIVE ACTION.

Plate XVIII:

Platoon in the Offensive Action.

No. 1.

No. 1 Section: Machine Gun Section.

No. 1. Fires Gun.
No. 2. Carries spare barrel and parts and assists No. 1.

No. 3. Ammunition carrier. No. 4. Scout and sniper. No. 5. Assistant do. No. 6., No. 7., No. 8. Ammunition carriers.	Plate XVIII. shows M.G. Section advancing from platoon in "artillery formation." Nos 4 and 5 (scouts) are not seen; they are in front, selecting position for gun.

No. 2.

In Plate XVIII. Machine Gun Section advancing in "artillery formation." In No. 2 you see the line advancing from the enemy point of view. Note the *six* men appear as *one*; narrow front to hostile fire.

No. 3.

The Machine Gun Section. Scout having given signa "Advance," the team move steadily forward. Commander then halts, views his position, and moves Nos. 1 and 2 forward to it; scouts pushing forward to select next position, also guarding the gun against surprise attack. Remainder well in rear with ammunition dump, No. 3 connecting file from gun to dump. When all ready, Section Leader sends message "All correct" to Platoon Commander, and under automatic fire of machine gun the platoon advances to final assault.

CHAPTER XX

GENERAL CONSIDERATIONS AND SUGGESTIONS

1. THE correct sequence of instruction must always be followed; the Official Handbook on the subject must be the model. This book follows on similar lines, and is the sequence taught in the Schools of Musketry.

Supervision by the machine gun officer, assisted by the senior N.C.O. or battalion sergeant-major instructor, who must maintain discipline among the instructors and learners.

2. **Mechanism.**—The proper sequence must always be insisted upon, and all gunners must be able to explain the working of the gun in their own words.

3. **Immediate Action and Stoppages** with stripping must be constantly practised, until gunners can apply the correct remedy almost by instinct.

4. **Gun Drill** needs constant reiteration, and must be done rapidly, but not at the expense of accuracy. It is not enough to know your gun technically—the "handling" must be clean and correct; this is absolutely essential.

5. **Points Before, During, and After Firing** must be frequently included in course of instruction.

6. **Care and Cleaning** can be taken with stripping.

7. Suggested Syllabus Chart for Instruction:

	First Hour.	*Second Hour.*	*Third Hour.*
1st day -	General description.	Stripping, with names of parts.	Mechanism, and care and cleaning.
2nd day -	Mechanism.	Gun drill.	Immediate action and stoppages.
3rd day -	Stripping and assembling.	Mechanism.	Points before, during, and after firing.

These tables can be prepared and altered, repeating more frequently any subject the section needs most.

Questions should be encouraged, but no time wasted.

8. **Lectures** on the following subjects, which must be short and interesting. Give time and thought to this work; it pays. All will tend to make the Hotchkiss gunners keen and regular in attendance, and keep alive their enthusiasm:—

(*a*) Organization. (*b*) Tactical handling of the gun. (*c*) Characteristics. (*d*) Methods of fire. (*e*) Cones and zones of fire. (*f*) Range finding.

9. Training out of doors, when weather conditions are favourable. A rough outline of work is suggested :—

(*a*) Indication and recognition of targets.

(*b*) Judging distances.

(*c*) Action from limbers. (With limbers loaded and packed, when marching along a road, positions can be taken up on both sides of a road in the shortest possible time.)

(*d*) Choice of gun positions. Points to observe:

(1) Concealment of firing position. (2) Good field of fire. (3) Movement between the ammunition dump and the gun—that it does not give the position away.

10. **Methods of Fire.**—Study this subject well; it affords endless satisfaction and fascination :—

(1) Horizontal traverse. (2) Vertical searching. (3) Swinging traverse. (4) Cones of fire. (5) Effective beaten zones of fire. (6) Bracketing fire. (7) Night firing.

11. **History of Guns.**—Keep a separate book with each gun, with its complete history, recording (1) date of issue; (2) all breakages, and parts replaced; (3) when and where gun was fired, and number of rounds fired; (5) in fact, anything interesting connected with the gun.

Plate XIX.

HOTCHKISS PORTABLE MACHINE GUN.

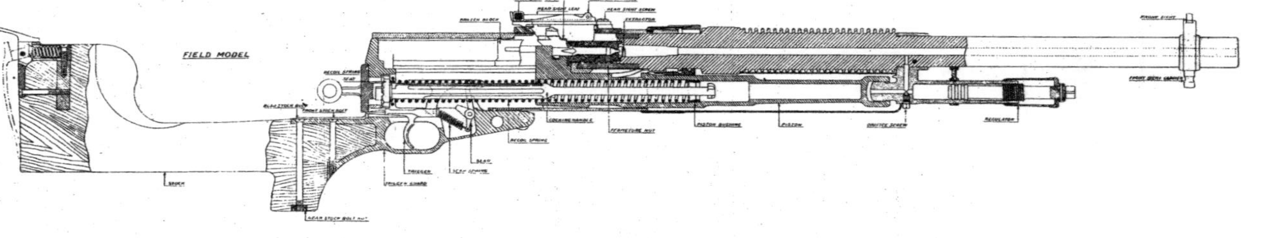

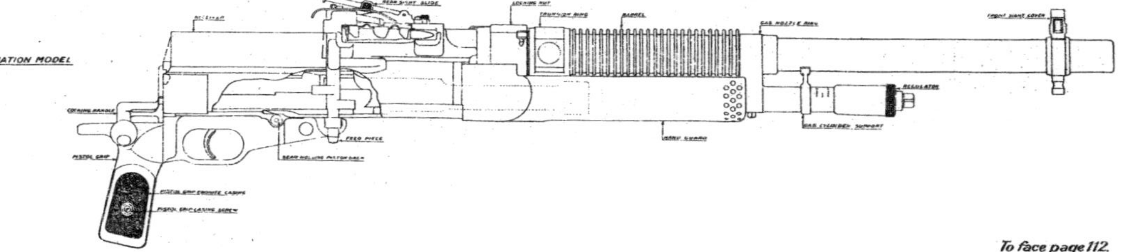

To face page 112.

www.ingramcontent.com/pod-product-compliance
Ingram Content Group UK Ltd.
Pitfield, Milton Keynes, MK11 3LW, UK
UKHW040015200726
13854UKWH00001B/218